SUPER SPORTS

John Allen
Ian Bamsey
Gordon Jones
Alan Lis
Ronnie Spain
Allan Staniforth

SUPER SPORTS

---

25 Years of classic
Mid - engine
Le Mans Coupes

A **FOULIS** Motoring Book

First published 1988

© **Miura Publications Ltd**

Published by
Haynes Publishing Group,
Sparkford, Near Yeovil, Somerset BA22 7JJ, England

Haynes Publications Inc.,
861 Lawrence Drive, Newbury Park, California, 91320, USA

Produced for G.T. Foulis & Co. Ltd by
Miura Publications Ltd
6, Foundry House, Stars Lane, Yeovil, Somerset BA20 1NL

The photographs are from the archives of LAT, London.

British Library Cataloguing in Publication Data

Various Authors
Super Sports - 25 Years of Classic Mid-Engine Le Mans Coupes
1. Racing Cars, 1964-1988
I. Title
629.2'28'0904

ISBN 0-85429-689-1

Library of Congress Catalog Card number 88-80557

Printed in England by:
Butler & Tanner Ltd, The Selwood Printing Works, Frome, Somerset

Artwork and Typesetting by:
Graphic Examples, Sherborne, Dorset

CONTENTS

INTRODUCTION

This book covers 25 years of Le Mans history (1964 - 1988) but does not attempt to chronicle the event: plenty of other publications have carried reports and results of the races. Rather, you will find here a celebration of 25 years of 'Super Sports' Le Mans cars. Of course, the term Super Sports is not an official racing car designation and in this context it is taken to mean those Mid-Engine Coupes which have challenged for outright victory in The Great 24 Hour Race.

The big capacity Mid-Engine Coupe was born in the early Sixties and the first of the genre to challenge for outright victory at Le Mans was the Ford GT40 of 1964. By 1965 a glory seeking Mid-Engine Coupe was either a brutish 7.0 litre stock block V8 Ford or a charismatic 4.0 litre thoroughbred V12 Ferrari and aerodynamics were tested as never before as the speed of the slippery projectiles soared over the 200m.p.h. mark. With three and a half miles flat out designers sought velocity without dangerous loss of stability and by 1971 a 600b.h.p. fully enclosed car was capable of 240mp.h. while remaining stable even through the notorious flat out kink in the seemingly endless chute.

At the end of 1971 engine power was slashed; international sports car racing was turned over to enclosed wheel Formula One cars. Somehow the spyder was nowhere near as stirring as the lamented fully enclosed sports racing car and the spyder years (1972 - 1979) were lean ones at Le Mans. Weak entries reflected a general dampening of enthusiasm for sports car racing which continued as the authorities tried replacing the spyders by production silhouette machines.

Thankfully the Automobile Club de L'Ouest had the right idea in the form of its GTP class out of which arose Group C. Rondeau set the ball rolling with victory at Le Mans for its GTP-inspired 1980 Mid-Engine Coupe. Subsequently the authorities opened all doors to the return of the fully enclosed Sports-Prototype, sparking an explosion of interest in sports car racing. Cars are invariably run at Le Mans for reasons which are fuelled by sheer enthusiasm and the enthusiast is inspired by the Mid-Engine Coupe. That infectious enthusiasm for the Super Sports Le Mans car brought about this book.

The core of the book is a series of special features, each giving a detailed insight into a different aspect of the Super Sports story. These features were specially commissioned and represent original research by acknowledged experts. Between them, the six authors have written over a dozen books on sports car racing. Each, however, is first and foremost an enthusiast inspired by the big capacity Mid-Engine Coupe.

The Super Sports car took many different guises over the first 25 years of its Le Mans history and this book presents them all. A series of double page spreads running throughout the work identifies all the Super Sports cars of the period. Each model is depicted and a pen portrait is painted by Alan Lis. A full index of Super Sports car coverage (with photograph identification) appears at the back of the book. The qualification for 'Super Sports' status has been taken, pre-1972 as a capacity of at least 2.5 litres, post 1981 as Group C1 or IMSA GTP trim (and including from intervening years the forerunners of the Group C cars).

This book is intended as a tribute to all those enthusiasts who helped field the cars that inspired it: to the designers, engineers, mechanics, helpers, team managers, car owners, sponsors, drivers and others whose enthusiasm enriched the Super Sports story. If that enthusiasm is transmittted through the pages of this book the efforts of the authors will not have been in vain.

BIRTH OF THE MID-ENGINE LE MANS COUPE

The principle of placing the engine between the driver's compartment and the rear wheels was not entirely new when it swept through international motor racing with the coming of the Sixties having been pioneered by off-beat racing cars as long ago as the 1920s. The Auto Union Grand Prix cars were famous pre-war exponents of the layout but suffered appalling suspension design and failed to set a trend.

The Auto Union was the brain child of Professor Ferdinand Porsche, one of the greatest automobile designers of all time and creator of the Volkswagen Beetle. When his son Ferdinand and daughter Louise founded the Porsche marque they did so converting Beetles into sports cars, 'hot rod' style and thus the Porsche sports car was born with its engine behind the rear axle. Porsche made its first Le Mans entry in 1951 with its rear engined sports coupe powered by a tuned 1100cc. Beetle engine producing a mere 40b.h.p.

The baby Porsche was reliable and won its class and for 1953 Porsche resolved to produce a proper small capacity sports-racing car. It did so by designing a tubular chassis and turning the drivetrain package around so that the engine was ahead of the rear axle in proper mid engine style. Thus was born the first post war coupe bodied mid engine sports-prototype.

That small capacity 1953 Porsche developed into the classic Types 550 and RS 2.0 litre sports-racing cars which were generally spyder bodied but often ran as coupes at Le Mans, careful wind cheating helping offset the power disadvantage of Porsche's own 1.5/2.0 litre four cylinder engine which retained the boxer configuration. Nevertheless, the big capacity mid engined Le Mans coupe did not appear until the early Sixties, by which time mid engine fever had swept the world of international motor racing following the efforts of Cooper and Lotus in Grand Prix racing.

Smaller frontal area, light weight and useful weight distribution had endowed the all independently sprung Cooper and Lotus chassis with sufficient performance on most circuits to offset the power disadvantage they had found themselves with. Ferrari had always enjoyed plenty of power and

had traditionally paid little heed to chassis technology. Jaguar had exploited that fact, running more aerodynamic cars at Le Mans in the mid Fifties to good effect.

At the end of the Fifties Carlo Chiti dragged Ferrari into the 'aerodynamic' era and introduced the first mid engine Ferrari racing cars. The Grand Prix and small capacity sports racers that first put a Ferrari engine behind the driver had V6 engines: Ferrari considered its V12 too long for a mid location.

The first of the new generation Ferrari sports racing car arrived at Le Mans in 1961: it was an enclosed wheel version of the contemporary (1.5 litre) Formula One car that set a 2.46 litre V6 behind the driver. The spyder-bodied '246SP' had won the '61 Targa Florio but was merely a back up at Le Mans to regular front engined 3.0 litre V12 Testa Rossa spyders.

The Ferrari 246SP faced a mid engined Maserati, the Tipo 63. This was a direct development of the existing Tipo 61, the famous 'Birdcage', rebuilt initially to set the 2.9 litre four cylinder engine behind the driver and with an independent rather than de Dion rear suspension. However, following disappointing early races Maserati shoehorned its V12 Grand Prix engine (enlarged from 2.5 to 3.0 litres) into the re-engineered spyder chassis for Le Mans.

In addition to one 246SP and three Tipo 63s, Le Mans '61 saw a mid engined 2.5 litre Cooper Monaco: like the 246SP, essentially an enclosed wheel Formula One car and again running a spyder body. None of the five new mid engine challengers lasted the race but the 246SP made its mark, running very strongly with the leading Testa Rossas.

Whereas Maserati returned to a proven front engined configuration for '62, the 246SP continued to impress and traded the Le Mans lead with the winning 4.0 litre Testa Rossa until its transmission broke. In addition to it Ferrari ran another mid engine spyder: the same chassis equipped with a less powerful 2.65 litre V8. A pointless exercise unless one considers the longer engine to have been a further step towards putting the V12 behind the driver.

The first ever fully enclosed large capacity mid engine car appeared at Le Mans in '62 in the form of the Tojeiro EE which ran a Coventry Climax four cylinder engine displacing 2495cc. Designed and constructed by renowned special builder John Tojeiro it had a space frame chassis and bodywork reminiscent of the Jaguar D type but surmounted by a coupe top with a rather flat, upright windscreen. Like the abandoned Tipo 63 and forgotton Cooper-Monaco, it was not destined to play a significant historical role, and retired with transmission failure.

By 1963 the 3.0 litre Testa Rossa engine had found its way into a wider track, longer wheelbase version of the V6/V8 chassis which sported a high windscreen body featuring an 'aerodynamic roll bar' shaped to deflect air towards the rear spoiler. The result was good grip and handling, a high top speed plus a reliable and highly competitive power output from the familiar V12. There was nothing to beat the '250P' at Le Mans in '63. Established early Sixties Le Mans rivals Maserati and Aston Martin countered with improved versions of their front engined coupes but the traditional sports car had met its match.

The 250P was not the only large capacity mid engine car at Le Mans in '63: there was also a turbine propelled Rover based on a BRM Formula One chassis with a 'roofless coupe' body style, and there was a Lola GT car. The Ford V8 propelled Lola Mk6 GT had an advanced aluminium monocoque chassis with independent suspension via wishbones and coil spring/dampers and a proper, aerodynamic coupe body and pointed the way to the future. For 1964 Ferrari would have a refined, coupe version of the 250P and Ford would have a development of the Lola-Ford in the GT40. The 'Supersports' big capacity, mid engine Le Mans coupe had been born.

WINGS & MONOCOQUES 1964 - 1971

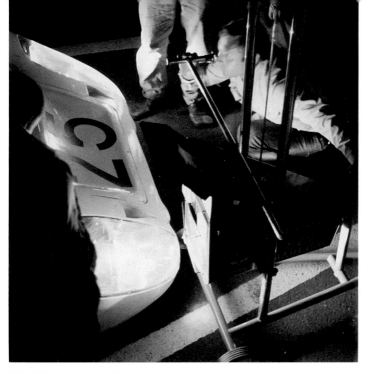

COLOUR PORTFOLIO
1964 - 1971

Page 9

The Howmet TX turbine car of Heppenstall/Thompson brought welcome variety to Le Mans in 1968, the first year after the monsters, but sadly it was rolled by Thompson, crashing out of the race.

Page 10 (top)

Headlamp adjustment for the Salzburg team Porsche 917 Langheck of Elford/Ahrens during the 1970 race. The JWA team refused to run the Langheck which was unwieldy in the corners but very fast on the straight.

Page 10 (middle)

The 1967 winning Ford MkIV of Gurney/Foyt chases the similar MkIV of McLaren (winner in '66) and Donohue off the Mulsanne straight and on towards Indianapolis: a race for which Gurney and Foyt were already famed.

Page 10 (bottom)

Rounding Mulsanne corner, in the twilight goes the 1966 Chaparral 2D of Bonnier/Hill. The car had recently won the Nurburgring ADAC 1000km. but was destined soon to fall out with electrical maladies.

Page 11

The Pescarolo/Servoz Gavin Matra leads a group of cars at the damp start in 1968. Behind, the Ford GT40 of Hawkins/Hobbs gets the jump on the similar car of team mates Rodriguez/Bianchi. Rodriguez/Bianchi went on to win.

Page 12

The Ford MkII of McLaren/Miles negotiates the Esses during the 1965 race, prior to becoming Ford's fifth retirement in only three hours of racing. The last Ford car dropped out within eight hours of the start.

Page 13

The Giunti/Galli Alfa Romeo T33/2 splashes through the long night en route to fourth place in 1968. The big bangers had gone, paving the way for a high result by Alfa Romeo's reliable 2.0 litre class challengers.

Page 13

Behind you! The JWA Porsche 917 Langheck of Siffert/Bell terrorises backmarkers during the 1971 race. Siffert had a lot of trouble with backmarkers in practice and at one stage was almost put off the road at high speed.

Page 14

The Schutz/Mitter Porsche 908, all hatches open, is prepared for the 1969 Le Mans race in the traditional Porsche base at Teloche. In the event the 3.0 litre car was rolled and caught fire and was a write-off.

Page 15

The essence of Les Vingt Quatre Heures du Mans is summed up by this night shot, taken during the 1969 running of the world's most famous endurance race. That year the closest ever win went to Ford over Porsche.

Page 15

The works Ferrari 512S of Posey/Bucknum heads for fourth place in 1970, passing the abandoned JWA Porsche 917 of Hobbs/Hailwood which looks about to get booked. In the background is the Alfa Romeo it collided with.

Page 16

The Siffert/Bell Porsche 917 Langheck leads the Vaccarrella/Juncadella Ferrari 512M and the Donohue/Hobbs Penske 512M through backmarkers into Terte Rouge early in the '71 race. Ahead is the sister JWA 917LH.

ALFA ROMEO TIPO 33

Autodelta, the competitions department of Alfa Romeo, was formed in 1964 under the direction of former Ferrari Technical Director Carlo Chiti. Initially it produced racing versions of the Milanese company's road going products. A front engined spaceframe coupe, the TZ appeared later and achieved some success in GT racing in the mid Sixties.

Early in 1967 a completely new mid engined prototype racer, the Tipo 33 was announced. It chassis was unusual in that it incorporated two parallel large diameter alloy tubes linked by a third to form an H-plan. A cast magnesium bulkhead linked the front of the parallel tubes and carried the wishbone front suspension. At the rear similarly conventional suspension was located by radius rods which picked up on a steel plated structure which was connected to the parallel tubes by a pair of magnesium beams which served as engine supports.

Ventilated disc brakes were fitted outboard at the front, inboard at the rear. Glassfibre bodywork offered a rounded nose with a single front opening to serve the water radiator with twin top exits ahead of a tall bulbous windscreen. The tail section curved over the rear wheels and terminated abruptly in a Kamm-type rear end. As raced in '67, the car was open roofed with a periscope for the fuel injected intake stacks appearing over the driver's left shoulder.

Power was provided by an alloy block four cam 1995cc. Alfa Romeo 90 degree V8 which was Lucas injected and was claimed to produce 260b.h.p. at 9,000r.p.m. However, the '67 season was spoilt by dreadful unreliability, in particular of the suspension and no real success was forthcoming. For '68 a new car was produced, still based on the H-frame chassis structure. The front suspension was strengthened and a new body design featured side mounted radiators and a detachable hard top. Also available was a 2.5 litre version of the V8 rated at 315b.h.p. at 8,800r.p.m.

On its debut in the Daytona 24 hour race

the Tipo 33/2 model enouragingly finished fifth, sixth and seventh overall taking the first three places in the 2.0 litre class. Further good results followed using both 2.0 and 2.5 litre engines. For Le Mans four works entries were backed by two privateer cars, all running the 2.0 litre engine and the factory cars having a long tail option which sported small vertical fins at the rear. Although one example was lost to fuel pump failure and both private entries dropped out, the surviving cars finished fourth, fifth and sixth overall, sweeping the 2.0 litre class.

By 1969 the Tipo 33/2 had been produced in sufficient numbers to gain homologation as a Group Four sports car and Autodelta turned its attention to the development of an open topped 3.0 litre prototype. Despite encouraging testing the factory withdrew its Le Mans entries but the Belgian Racing Team VDS upheld Alfa Romeo honour in the 24 hour classic with one 2.5 litre and one 2.0 litre car. Alas, the bigger capacity coupe went out with a broken oil line after only four hours while its long tail sister car crashed in the eighth hour. By 1970 the Tipo 33/2's career was over, brute power dominating sports-prototype racing.

ALFA ROMEO	
Tipo 33/2 - 1969	90 degree V8
Alloy semi-monocoque	2.5 litres
Suspension:	Alloy block
wishbone front	Fuel injected
wishbone rear	32 valves
Engine semi-stressed	d.o.h.c.
Alfa Romeo gearbox	Unblown
Flat bottom	315 b.h.p.

LOLA T70 ASTON MARTIN

At the end of 1966 Aston Martin announced a completely new V8 engine design to power a coupe version of Eric Broadley's Lola T70 chassis that had recently won the Can Am Series driven by John Surtees.

The engine was an alloy block five litre unit with a bore and stroke of 98 x 84mm alloy cylinder heads with hemi-spherical combustion chambers and double overhead camshafts per bank. A nitrided steel crankshaft was mounted on five main bearings while ignition on the dry sump unit was by Lucas and initially it ran on four Weber carburettors. The chassis was a light alloy sheet monocoque with integral fuel tanks and carried double wishbone suspension with coil spring/damper units feeding loadings into steel reinforced sections. A five speed Hewland LG600 gearbox transmitted the British V8 power through 10 x 15 inch rear wheels, 8 x 15 inch rims being fitted at the front. Girling 12.5 inch ventilated disc brakes were mounted outboard, proud of the wheels to aid cooling.

For the Le Mans test weekend in April 1967 one T70 appeared and recorded an encouraging third fastest time after aerodynamic changes.

On its racing debut at the Nurburgring the Lola-Aston Martin sported Lucas fuel injection and qualified second only to retire after a suspension breakage. A second chassis was prepared for Le Mans and was used by Surtees and Hobbs, the original being passed on to Irwin and De Klerk. With knowledge gained at the test weekend the newer car was fitted with a more streamlined tail section with adjustable spoiler across the rear. Surtees started thirteenth in the echelon, Irwin twenty fifth. The race was a disaster. Surtees lasted a mere three laps before a piston was holed while Irwin retired after less than an hour with a cracked damper on his Aston Martin engine's crankshaft.

Chevrolet power was used in subsequent races, Aston Martin withdrawing from racing.

LOLA	ASTON MARTIN
T70 - 1967	90 degree V8
Alloy monocoque	5.0 litres
Suspension:	Alloy block
wishbone front	Fuel injected
wishbone rear	16 valves
Engine semi-stressed	d.o.h.c.
Hewland gearbox	Unblown
Flat bottom	460 b.h.p.

LOLA T70 CHEVROLET

Customer versions of the alloy and steel monocoque Type 70 coupe were produced by Lola Cars with the intention of gaining Group 4 status. Regulation changes for the 1968 season restricted engines to a maximum of 5.0 litres and then only in Group 4, Lolas having been raced with engines of various sizes during 1967. The 4995cc Chevrolet V8 used by many teams was prepared by Traco Engineering of Culver City California and was reputed to produce around 425bhp depending on the use of either Lucas fuel injection, Holley or Weber carburettors. Engine apart, the 1968 Type 70 Mk 3's were replicas of the previous year's Aston Martin engined Le Mans cars.

No works Lolas ran in 1968, customer cars in the hands of drivers of the calibre of Bonnier, Gardener and reigning world champion Hulme upholding the honour of the Huntingdon marque. The Le Mans organisers received two Lola entries, a Swedish Sportscars Unlimited chassis for Norinder/Axeisson and a British Jackie Epstein entered car for the entrant and Nelson. Qualified conservatively in among the 2 litre class leaders, both cars suffered terminal engine failures in the race.

For 1969 bodywork and internal revisions constituted a new car in all but type number. The T70 Mk3B had a more pronounced wedge shaped nose, widened rear spoiler and front-hingeing doors. Despite domestic domination in British sprint events and a fortunate Daytona win to its credit, only a single example was entered at the 1969 Le

Mans race. The Scuderia Fillipinetti car, driven by Bonnier/Gregory, qualified 11th. During the opening hours it ran reliably in the top ten but then it was slowed by cracked cylinder heads which were eventually replaced, as were gaskets, valves and brake discs. Having spent three hours stationary in the pits the hard work of the mechanics was to prove to be of no avail as the engine blew on the Mulsanne straight shortly after midnight when Gregory was at the wheel.

Lola was represented at the 1970 race by the Belgian Racing Team VDS Mk3B of Pilette/Gosselin which was fitted with a Bonnier-Morand tuned engine. Overshadowed by the Porsche versus Ferrari duel ahead, the car retired with clutch failure.

The same car returned in 1971 to give the T70 its Le Mans swansong. The driver pairing was unaltered, their luck unfortunately was even worse, the Belgian team posting the first retirement with a broken piston after barely one hour.

LOLA	CHEVROLET
T70 - 1968	90 degree V8
Alloy monocoque	5.0 litres
Suspension:	Iron block
wishbone front	Carburettor
wishbone rear	16 valves
Engine semi-stressed	Pushrod
Hewland gearbox	Unblown
Flat bottom	425 b.h.p.

THE SAD CAR

The Lola T70 coupe was a fine chassis in search of a good strong engine. It started its Le Mans career with the Aston Martin V8: a disaster. Thereafter came variations on the Chevrolet V8 theme, without success. Gordon Jones looks at the T70 Le Mans cars and finds much to be admired in their chassis engineering.

As an exercise to win Le Mans, the Lola-Aston Martin project was an unmitigated disaster. It brought no kudos to any of the involved parties. It did nothing for the Lola and Aston Martin names that both cars should fail miserably on their much heralded Le Mans outing. It did nothing for the people involved. For Eric Broadley of Lola, it meant much time and effort expended for nil return. For John Surtees as the development and race driver, a wasted six months. For Tadek Marek, the talented Aston Martin engine designer, the creation that was to have been his 'magnum opus' just before retirement, became his crucifix. The engine had to be totally redesigned, thereby losing Aston Martin two years before the release of the first DBSV8, and probably therefore contributed to the demise of the David Brown Aston Martin era. If any good came from the debacle, one can only say that the redesigned V8 became the backbone of Aston Martin power for the next decade.

The project had started back in the early 1960's. Aston Martin knew that its six cylinder engine was reaching the limits of development. Tadek Marek, a brilliant Polish engineer and winner of the 1939 Polish Grand Prix, had escaped to Britain in 1941, and John Wyer, as the new General Manager at Aston's, had poached him from the British Motor Corporation. Marek designed a brand new V8 engine; a 90 degree vee of 96mm bore x 83mm stroke giving 4806cc, with chain driven double overhead camshafts and four twin choke Weber carburettors. The whole engine was cast from aluminium alloy; block, crankcase, sump, heads, camshaft covers and inlet manifolds. The cylinder bores had top seated wet liners in cast iron, and the five main bearing caps were in steel.

With Aston Martin's penchant for race development, the new V8 engine was to have run in the 1963 Le Mans. A new Development Project car had been designed, the DP215, but with the V8 not race ready, the Marque ran an enlarged version of the six cylinder engine and achieved an incredible 198.6 mph on the Mulsanne straight during practice. After Le Mans, an internal economy drive closed down the Experimental and the Racing departments and the V8 development was shelved. The project had to be resurrected in 1966, since shoehorning the enlarged six cylinder engines into the DB4 was becoming extremely difficult.

The V8 engine was given a new development project number, DP218, and the bore was enlarged from 96mm to 98mm, giving a swept volume of 5008cc, not 5064cc as reported in most contemporary articles. Aston, true to its principles, still wished to test the new V8 in racing. Eric Broadley's 1963 Lola coupe with V8 power, and his subsequent Ford GT40 creation had impressed many people, especially John Wyer. Since then, the 1965 Lola T70 spyder had acquitted itself well, and Aston Martin was just one of many who approached Broadley and suggested that he produce a new coupe. Aston Martin wanted to test the new V8 at the most prestigious race in the book, Le Mans. Success at Le Mans brings fat order books, and Aston Martin had been sliding backwards since its 1959 Le Mans wins.

A deal was struck. A Lola coupe, the Aston Martin V8 engine, and arguably the best development driver of the era to form Lola Racing to run the new car at Le Mans 1967. The second 1966 works Lola T70 MKII spyder was given to Aston Martin as a development hack. The Aston engine sat nicely in the T70 chassis, with minimal alteration to the rear pontoon chassis members. The V8 engine came through the test with flying colours, and Aston Martin returned the T70 spyder to Team Surtees in August to await the coupe.

The first coupe came off the production line on 2 November 1966. The Lola T70 GT had to be offered for sale by Lola with V8 Chevrolet engines as standard, or Ford and Aston Martin V8s as options. Therefore John Surtees started chassis development at Goodwood with a 5.5 litre V8 Chevrolet prepared by Los Angeles tuner Ryan Falconer. These engines were producing around 460 bhp and were therefore comparable to the 450bhp that Aston was claiming with its V8 on carburetters.

After the Racing Car Show in early January 1967, the car was fitted with the Aston Martin engine. A test programme at Goodwood in February, which included twelve and fourteen hour endurance runs, was deemed successful, and the Le Mans project was given the green light. The Aston engine was rather heavy and the engineers aimed to develop a fuel injection version to provide more horse power. The programme was first the Le Mans Test Weekend for carburetter and fuel injection back to back testing, a proving race at the Nurburgring 1000 kms, then a two car assault on Le Mans.

Eric Broadley had designed the Lola T70 MK III as a development of the MKII spyder; lighter chassis, improved suspension, better brakes, an improved gear linkage, driver cooling, ease of maintenance, and a revolutionary feature - one chassis that could be either spyder or GT coupe.

The chassis was a light alloy and sheet steel welded and riveted monocoque, common today, but highly original when the first T70 spyder was built. The front suspension was hung on a box section extension, with the rear suspension and transaxle on twin box sections on either side of the engine. Torsional rigidity was provided by light alloy transverse bulkheads. The suspension was by double wishbones on self-aligning roller bearing and ball joints with telescopic shock absorbers and co-axial coil springs.

The front wishbones were, again by current design, very conventional. Top links were short adjustable machined steel bar with the same for the bottom trailing link, but using a fabricated arm for the main lower arm. The coil spring damper unit was fixed to the top of the front transverse bulkhead and acted on this lower arm, as did the high mounted anti-roll bar. Steering was by stock BMC rack and pinion set high behind the front axle and linked to rear facing steering arms.

The very large, 12 1/2" diameter ventilated brake discs developed by Girling from the Kelsey Hayes design sat tight against the front uprights, with large offset hub carriers

First run for the Lola-Aston Martin at Le Mans was during the test weekend for the '67 race. This is the fuel injected engine.

24

to leave the discs and their forward facing double calipers in the air stream. The magnesium wheels were located on six large diameter pins, and secured with a single large knock-on three eared nut. The rear upright, a large three eared casting, was suspended by reverse wishbones at the bottom and short top link located on the rear transverse bulkhead. The forward half of the top wishbone and the lower radius rod located forward at the centre transverse bulkhead, just behind the driver. As at the front, the anti-roll bar acted on the lower wishbones. Also the rear wheels were well offset on the upright, and the inboard disc brakes sat in the cooling airstream.

The wheels were 15" with rims designed initially at 8" front and 10" rear for 10.60 x 15 and 12.00 x 15 Firestone tyres. However, to promote more straight line speed on the Mulsanne straight, the fronts were reduced to 9.20 x 15 for Le Mans. Wheelbase was 7'11", track 4'10" and ground clearance with driver, 25 litres of oil, 15 litres of water and 170 litres of fuel was 4". All up weight was between 1750 and 1800 lbs, according to source, making the Lola-Aston a heavy-weight when compared with the Ferraris.

The body was self coloured, carbon filament reinforced glass fibre by Specialised Mouldings. The works car was finished in a very dark green with white Team Surtees arrow edged with red. LOLA-ASTON MARTIN was painted in white on each scuttle. The body had been translated from a "back of a fag packet" sketch by Eric Broadley and Peter Jackson of Specialised Moulding. The stylist who achieved the final wind cheating design was a New Zealand named Jim Clark.

The quarter sphere windscreen was bonded in with eight-hour epoxy, to make it a stressed member of the central body section, and to ensure a smooth airflow, without the usual rubber grommet. Doors were gullwing style with a positive handle lock both inside and outside. Both front and rear body panels were easily removeable. A spare wheel sat upright across the tail to satisfy the regulations. The gearbox was yet another new item, the first T70 coupe carrying the very first Hewland LG600 five speed box.

On April 8 and 9 1967 the first coupe went to Le Mans for the Test Weekend. The car was still fitted with the carburetter engine, since finance had delayed the fuel injected unit. However despite many problems, the team was well pleased with the results. Third fastest lap time in the dry, behind the two Ferrari P4's and faster than both the MKII Ford GT40 and the Ford MKIV. However, this was undoubtedly due to Surtees and the chassis, since the car only pulled a disappointing 186 mph down the Mulsanne straight when Ford and Ferrari were both over the magic 200 mph mark.

Surtees said that the engine would not pull more than 6000 rpm. The Aston Martin engineers considered that this must be caused by the shape of Lola T70 tail spoiling the airflow. Was the air passing over the carbs too quickly, or was the shape of the tail causing turbulance? Both would deny air to the carburetters, and all sorts of changes were tried; different intake trumpets, cover plates over and around the intakes, different exhaust systems ejecting at different parts of the tail. Nothing changed the problem, and the engine still ran hot.

Nurburgring 1000 kms on 28 May 1967 and a lone Lola - Aston Martin entered. The ADAC gave it race number 1 in honour of the occasion. The Lucas fuel-injection engine was now fitted. This was the shake-down for Le Mans, just two weeks away. The big spoilered tail from the Le Mans test weekend was gone, replaced with the original prototype rear deck. The Chaparral 2F claimed pole, but Surtees was second, and within his own 1966 Ferrari lap record! The car was sidelined in the race when a rear wishbone broke.

Two cars arrived at Le Mans. The prototype, Nurburgring car, No 112, for Chris Irwin and South African Peter de Klerk. A new chassis, No 11, for John Surtees and David Hobbs. This latter car had a new rear deck. Gone was the carb intake trough and upswept rear side decks. Instead a large perspex window covering the whole rear deck, with a full width adjustable 'flipper' aerofoil across the tail. The regulations demanded that during the race the spare wheel had to be taken from the car, placed on the pit counter, and then replaced in the car. Lola achieved this with speed by stowing the rear wheel horizontally, such that it could be withdrawn through the large tail aperture without opening the rear bodywork! The other advantage of this was to allow the megaphone exhaust exits to be placed low down and centrally to avoid the turbulent air higher up the tail.

Both cars had the fuel injection engines, with ignition by Scintilla Magnetos. Practice was again troublesome with continuous engine problems. Both engines were running hot. The Irwin/de Klerk car required

water every couple of laps and frequent new head gaskets, and the Surtees/Hobbs car was down on power, and finally blew a head gasket.

These problems did nothing for morale. Worse, there were two teams, with Lola engineers looking after the car, and Aston Martin engineers looking after the engine. Blame was soon being apportioned, and irritability turned to acrimony. After practice, the Lola mechanics looking over the car claimed that the Lucas fuel injection was 180 degrees out of phase. The final straw for the Aston Engineers was a race sponsorship deal by Surtees to fit Marchal sparking plugs instead of the Champion plugs that had been used throughout the preceeding months.

In the race Surtees rushed off from thirteenth on the grid to seventh by the end of the first lap, only to retire on the third lap with a holed piston. Chris Irwin was in and out of the pits every other lap until he too retired. The Lucas fuel injection pump was tightening up, causing the drive belt to fly off. Then the oil pressure fell as the engine got hotter, and it was eventually running so roughly that the crankshaft vibration damper shattered.

The Aston Martin engineers claimed that the problems were due solely to Surtees changing the plugs. Surtees doubted the horsepower claimed by Aston, and could substantiate the statement by comparison with the known 450 bhp of the Chevrolet unit. When the Aston Martin engineers stripped the engines after Le Mans they found them totally 'cooked'.

The cylinder heads were distorted, and even the alloy blocks had twisted making the cylinder bores oval. Even the steel main bearing caps were distorted. With hindsight, and when emotions had cooled, both teams agreed that the real problem had been a lack of finance. A miniscule budget, Surtees recalls it at only £21,000, meant that not enough time had been put into development and testing.

The Lola T70-Chevrolet was never a success at Le Mans, though the chassis was effective and the American V8 engine pumped out an honest 450b.h.p.

26

The Aston Martin adventure was over but the Lola T70 lived on. The Le Mans race was moved from June to the end of September in 1968, to avoid the French elections, which would have seriously depleted the gate. Two T70's entered the race; Jackie Epstein and bearded Swede Ulf Norinder. Both cars were standard production T70 MkIII coupes with Chevrolet V8 engines, and had been campaigned all year around the European Group 4 races.

Epstein's car was in fact the same chassis that Surtees had driven at Le Mans in 1967, but gone was the Aston Martin engine, replaced with a Chevrolet. Both cars were running smaller 4940 cc units, specially prepared for the 24 hours. The engines were fitted with four Weber carburetters and Autolite plugs, and despite their detuned stake, were still producing around 450 bhp.

Both cars had Hewland LG600 five speed gearboxes and used Firestone tyres. In fact, the only differences were the Castrol stickers on the Epstein car, the Esso stickers on the Norinder car and their weights. The Norinder car was lighter at 973 kg with the Epstein car scaling 986 kg. Sadly, the Norinder/Axelsson car ran out of fuel during the fifth hour and was disqualified, but the Epstein/Nelson car ran well until the transmission failed after seventeen hours.

Although homologated into Group 4 on the basis that it was a development of the MkIII, and from a theme or concept point of view, that is true, the 1969 Mark IIIB GT was in fact a totally new design, with all new parts. Designed at the same time as the F5000 T142, the IIIB used all the same running gear. It was not a sister to the T160 as commonly reported.

The chassis was now an all alloy bonded and riveted monocoque. The transverse bulkheads were stiffer and the rear chassis hoop incorporated a detachable cast magnesium cross member. Torsional rigidity was up to 5000 lbs. ft. per degree.

The bodywork by Specialised Mouldings was now sleeker than before, although some have said that the new 'droop-snoot'

made the car look sad! The comment alone is an interesting aside on our propensity for applying human, and frequently feminine attributes to objects that we love and describe as beautiful.

The roll-over bar was bonded into the cockpit roof section, with a quarter sphere laminated windscreen bonded in as before. Doors were now hinged forward. The gullwing design of the MkIII had given no advantages and was by its nature of heavier construction and more difficult to open quickly. Surtees had a gullwing door lift and blow off at the Le Mans Test Weekend in 1967 despite the positive locking system. Front and rear body sections were quickly removeable as before.

Eric Broadley had retained his proven twin wishbone suspension set-up on self aligning roller bearing and ball joints. Co-axial springs were fitted with adjustable Koni shock absorbers.

The ventilated disc brakes were now standard, the 12" x 1.1" discs being mounted on light alloy bells with aluminium four pot full area thick pad calipers. "Redman" couplings were fitted on the brake bells to improve disc life. Despite the Mark III design setting calipers and discs well into the air stream, it was found necessary to provide special cooling ducts through the bodywork onto the brakes. Wheels were still 15" diameter cast magnesium, with 8", 10", 11" and 12.5" front rims, and 10", 14" and a massive 17" rear rim without changes to suspension or bodywork. Track varied with rim width from 57" down to 54" for the widest tyres, but the wheelbase remained as for the Mark III at 95".

The standard engine option was a TRACO built and tuned 304.6 cu. in. V8 Chevrolet. The engine specification included four bolt main bearing caps; fully counterbalanced crankshaft; light alloy flywheel; forged pistons; heavy duty connecting rods; ported, flowed and polished cylinder heads; special valves; double valve springs; light alloy rockers on needle roller bearings; high lift race camshaft with roller followers; four 48 mm downdraught Weber

carburetters and a dry sump lubrication system.

Transmission was still via the Hewland LG600 five speed transaxle and roller spline driveshafts. New for 1969 was a redesigned crown wheel and pinion following a few failures in 1968. The clutch was a Borg and Beck 7.25", three plate unit.

Flexible fuel cells were incorporated into the monocoque structure, with a large single filler arranged for rapid filling. Some teams fitted a large filler on each side. A surge tank was mounted at the rear of the car, incorporating a non-return valve. Fuel feed was by two Bendix electric fuel pumps.

Water was cooled by a fully ducted radiator at the front, and oil by two light alloy coolers, ducted and mounted on the centre bulkhead. A lightweight Varley dry battery provided power for short races, with provision for a large capacity lead acid battery for long distance racing. A Lucas alternator was mounted on the gearbox. The four headlights were fitted in vertical pairs behind a long perspex nose fairing.

Weight of the first car was about 860 kilograms, including oil and water, but the cars were to be homologated at 800 kilos.

Two Lola T70 Mark IIIB coupes ran at Le Mans. In 1969 the Scuderia Filipinetti entry driven by Jo Bonnier and American Masters Gregory showed considerable speed round the circuit, however the Louis Morand 4995cc Chevrolet failed in the thirteenth hour.

In 1970 and 1971 Count van der Straaten's Dutch racing team took their ex John Woolfe Lola to Le Mans with Pilette and Gosselin as drivers. In 1970 running the smaller 4940cc engine, they ran well until the tenth hour when reports tell us that the gearbox failed. In 1971 they reverted to the standard 4995cc engine, which let them down after only three hours.

The Lola T70-Chevrolet found 24 hour success at Daytona rather than Le Mans. Prepared and entered by Roger Penske's highly professional team, this example won the 1969 Daytona race.

CHAPARRAL 2D CHEVROLET

Based at Midland, West Texas, Chaparral Cars was virtually a clandestine R and D department of General Motors. Proprietor Jim Hall produced a series of open top, Chevrolet engined sports cars for the United States Road Racing Championship between 1963 and 1965, incorporating many innovations - such as automatic transmissions and glass fibre reinforced plastic chassis. The cars were developed to a sufficient pitch for Hall to win the national title in 1965. Among his race wins was a victory over the works Ferrari and Ford teams at the Sebring 12 Hours: this led to General Motors backing a World Manufacturers Championship campaign in 1966.

The car used was designated the 2D: in effect it was the 1965 Sebring winning machine with a coupe top. The chassis dated back to 1963 and was a monocoque in GRP with steel crossmembers carrying suspension components: wishbones at the front, radius arms, lower wishbones and single top links at the rear. Coil spring/damper units were, of course, fitted front and rear. Hall's special relationship with GM enabled utilisation of lightweight all aluminium engines of 5.36 litres producing in excess of 400 bhp at 7000 rpm. A hydraulic torque converter transmitted the power to a three speed automatic gearbox. Outwardly the 2D was distinguished by a periscopic air collector scoop on the cockpit roof which fed the carburettors. A rear air dam was balanced by the venting of the nose mounted radiator into the low pressure area ahead of the windscreen, reducing frontal lift as well as rear.

On its European debut, the 2D scored a surprise victory at the Nurburgring driven by Bonnier/Phil Hill. The team went to Le Mans with high expectations. A rude awakening awaited it, the car retiring with electrical problems after only five hours racing.

CHAPARRAL	CHEVROLET
2D - 1966	90 degree V8
G.r.p. monocoque	5.4 litres
Suspension:	Alloy block
wishbone front	Carburettor
wishbone rear	16 valves
Engine semi-stressed	Push rod
GM gearbox	Unblown
Flat bottom	440 b.h.p.

CHAPARRAL 2F CHEVROLET

For the 1967 season the Chaparral 2D chassis was fitted with a 7.0 litre V8 engine, increasing power by around 100 bhp. The car was radically altered in the aerodynamic department, a new slab sided body of resin coated PVC foam covering many internal changes. The radiators were mounted high on the flanks, angled forwards ahead of the rear wheels, hot air exiting through apertures in the upper rear deck. The 2D's distinctive air scoop was discarded, the engine drawing breath from the low pressure area beneath the large rear suspension mounted aerofoil that dominated the car. Developed on the 2E Can-Am car during 1966, the "flipper" was hydraulically operated by a foot pedal which held the blade flat in the minimum drag position when depressed by the driver, springing into the maximum drag configuration when released. Balancing out this device was a wide opening feeding air into the nose of the car which contained a spring loaded trap door through which air would be dumped at speeds in excess of 140 mph.

Automatic transmission was again used with internal components strengthened to cope with greater loadings from the more powerful engine. Despite encouraging performances in early races, it became clear that the transmission was not up to the job. The team entered two cars for the 1967 Le Mans race after a series of retirements from the preceeding rounds of the Manufacturers Championship. Hill and Spence qualified second fastest a mere 0.3 seconds off "pole". Both cars were delayed at the start as the drivers fastened their seatbelts as instructed. Spence climbed to second place after two hours. Then just before midnight, a problem with the aerofoil operating mechanism locked it in the "braking" position, seriously affecting top speed. Despite this, the car remained in touch with the leaders and got back into third place

before the inevitable transmission failure occured. Three hours were lost as a rebuild was carried out in the pits. On its return to the race the car lapped quickly but lasted barely another hour before transmission gremlins put it out for good. The second car of Jennings/Johnson was driven more conservatively but succumbed to difficulties with its starter and battery after seven hours.

The rule changes at the end of the 1967 season outlawed the Chaparral, Hall and his team returning to the States to lead the fight against McLaren in the Can Am Series.

CHAPARRAL	CHEVROLET
2F - 1967	90 degree V8
G.r.p. monocoque	7.0 litres
Suspension:	Iron block
wishbone front	Carburettor
wishbone rear	16 valves
Engine semi-stressed	Pushrod
GM gearbox	Unblown
Flat bottom	530 b.h.p.

FERRARI 275LM

Directly descended from the 246SP, the first mid engined Ferrari V12 sports car, the 275P, was conceived as a multi-tubular spaceframe chassis with independent suspension of double wishbones and coil spring/dampers fore and aft. It was used during the 1963 season as the '250P' prior to the fitting of a larger and more powerful engine. For 1964 a twin cam, two valve 60 degree V12 with a bore and stroke of 77 x 58.8mm was used. Displacing 3285cc, 320 bhp was claimed as the output at 7700 rpm, using six twin choke Weber carburettors. The chassis was clothed in the now classic beaten aluminium body designed by Pininfarina which featured an aerodynamically styled roll over hoop, to help stabilise the airflow over the rear bodywork.

A coupe version of the 275P was intended for homologation into the 1964 Grand Touring car category but insufficient examples were fully built for it to be allowed to race as a G.T. model outside of Italy, precipitating a major row between Ferari and the C.S.I. which spilled over into Grand Prix racing.

The 275LM was never run as a works car, rather becoming a mainstay of the private entrant in the mid-sixties, scoring many lesser Prototype victories. However, there was also a surprise win at Le Mans in 1965. In a race which had seen a head on clash between the factory Ferrari and Ford teams, the intensity of the battle caused the retirement of all the works cars leaving victory to the North American Racing Team 275LM of Rindt and Gregory.

275LMs continued to appear at Le Mans long after their prime, eventually enjoying 'Group 4' homologation. They performed with distinction, Piper and Attwood guiding the former's British Racing Green example to seventh place in 1968 while the N.A.R.T. car returned to the Sarthe circuit in 1969 and in the hands of Posey/Zeccoli finished an honourable ninth.

FERRARI	
275LM - 1964	60 degree V12
Steel spaceframe	3.3 litres
Suspension:	Alloy block
wishbone front	Carburettor
wishbone rear	24 valves
Engine unstressed	d.o.h.c
Ferrari gearbox	Unblown
Flat bottom	320 b.h.p.

THE BELIEVER

Ferrari had little time for the 275LM. Its intended '64 GT car was homologated by the Italian authorities only to be shelved by the CSI on a technicality. Running as a make-weight prototype, it won the 1965 Le Mans race by accident. Thereafter, only David Piper had time for the outmoded machine. John Allen asked Piper what he saw in it.

By 1968, when the CSI's new rules for sports car racing were introduced, the Ferrari 275LM was struggling to keep its head above water in international events. Its competition debut had been made way back in 1964, but, unlike the GT40, which made its first race appearance only three months after the LM, the LM's development had been minimal, and Ferrari had expended little effort on keeping it competitive. Only 32 examples were built, but despite this number being 18 less than required, from 1966 the car was homologated as a sports car. In minor events it proved for some years to be quite competitive, but in major events it was hard pressed to better its old rival the GT40, and its frontline career included only one really significant win - in 1965 at Le Mans, the circuit for which it had beeen named. Victory there was obtained only after the works Ferrari P2s and the Ford GTs had driven each other into the ground.

As a tool for an enthusiastic private entrant, the 250LM (this colloquial title was something of a misnomer, for all but the first example were fitted from new with the 275 engine) still provided an interesting contender for overall victory in national and non-championship international races. The history of the LM at Le Mans began in 1964, when two cars were entered; the following year, the tally was five, sufficient to garner the first two places for the marque. Only one ran there in 1966, but it retired when a head gasket blew. By 1967 the number of LMs at the start was precisely zero, and the type's Le Mans history would almost certainly have come to a halt there and then had not the CSI decided, with effect from the start of the next season, to ban all the big-engined prototypes. With their LMs suddenly made more competitive, the privateers flocked to Le Mans in 1968, and four of Ferrari's old warhorses

found their way to the startline for the 36th Grand Prix d'Endurance.

Out of 53 qualifiers, the four LMs were surprisingly closely grouped, occupying 27th, 28th, 29th and 32nd places on the grid. David Piper's pea-green car, which he shared with Dickie Attwood, was 28th, with a time of 4m 02.0s, a long way behind the best Group 4 qualifier, the Rodriguez/Bianchi GT40, which clocked 3m39.8seconds, for fourth spot.

Piper's car was unquestionably the most advanced LM at the event. Its chassis number, 8165, gives it away as being the final 250LM built, being delivered to Scuderia Filipinetti in early 1966, and making only one race appearance - at the Nurburgring - with that team. By 1967 most owners of LMs had given up the struggle to keep their cars competitive, and had sold them to make way for somethinig newer; Piper's attitude was that the 250LM could be made to work, given the right amount of well-directed effort; he bought 8165 from Filipinetti, and added various non-standard features to the ones it already possessed. Effectively, Piper had been at the forefront of 250LM development, and he more than anyone was responsible for the car being as competitive as it was.

Much of Piper's development work concerned wheel and tyre improvements, for the mid-sixties saw the American tyre companies becoming involved, producing wide slick tyres that transformed motor racing. Appendix C regulations allowed the fitting of replacement wider wheels on a car, because the slicks could not be used on wire wheels, which were likely to break up under the cornering forces generated. Initially, both the GT40 and the 250LM used Borrani wires and Dunlop tyres, but it soon became totally impractical to race these cars on Dunlop rubber, complete with the inner tubes required because of the nature

of wire wheels.

Piper had a contract with Dunlop, which initially worked well. However, eventually the stage was reached where, even if the LM qualified in pole pcsition for, say, a race at Brands Hatch and led for a couple of laps, it would eventually go more and more slowly and be passed by almost everybody. In the hope of getting out from under the Dunlop contract, Piper contacted Dunlop's Dick Jeffries, who agreed that if Piper could prove to Dunlop's technicians Alex Maskell and Rick Barlow that the tyres were not competitive, Dunlop would release Piper from his contract.

A visit to Brands Hatch followed, and Piper showed the Dunlop technicians that their tyres were no match for the latest American offerings. Dunlop was as good as its word, and Piper was released from his contract, turning instead to Firestone rubber. The new tyres, which were tubeless so as to reduce unsprung weight, had to be run on wider rims, but as for obtaining any the Ferrari factory was less than helpful; the LM had been homologated on 6-inch front wheels and 7.5-inch rears, and Ferrari maintained that if bigger wheels and slicks were put onto the car, the gearbox would break. It rarely did.

One requirement connected with new wheel and tyre combinations was that the car's track had to be kept the same as homologated, so any outboard increase in wheel width had to be matched by an equivalent increase inboard. This was something of a problem, for there was not much room to widen the wheels towards the centre of the car, without having them touch the rear springs. Piper designed his own wheels for the LM, and had patterns made in Modena, for the wheels to be cast by ATS. At the front they were 10 inches wide, and at the rear, 14.5 inches for the dry weather versions, 12.5 inches for the wet.

On the first occasion the new wheels were used, at Silverstone, the LM went through scrutineering without problem, but when the GT40s were scrutineered, they were not so fortunate. John Wyer had provided new wheels for the GT40s but had neglected to ensure that the track remained unchanged; most of the extra width had gone outwards, where it was accommodated in flared wheel arches. After scrutineering, John Wyer and John Eason-Gibson, the Secretary of the BRDC, went to see Piper, to request that he refrain from protesting the GT40s' illegal wheels - on the grounds that if he did, there would be hardly anyone left in the race. Piper was decidedly unhappy about the whole affair, pointing out that on a fraction of JW's budget Piper had managed to get it right, and had gone to considerable lengths to ensure that his wheels were legal.

Being irate can help to get the adrenalin flowing, and it was a very irate David Piper who strapped himself into the LM to take the start of that particular event. His anger was such that it enabled him to lead the race from start to finish, and resist all attempts by theoretically superior cars to get past.

Piper had many plans for 8165; despite it being a mere 3.3-litres pitted against the 4.7-litres of the Fords, the LM could hold its own against most of the GT40s, and really it was only the likes of Denny Hulme and Paul Hawkins who provided serious opposition for Piper's green LM. However, as 1967 progressed, Piper formulated plans which he intended would make the LM unbeatable; the key was to be supercharging. Existing rules at that time permitted cars to have their engines enlarged up to the maximum of the category in which a car was homologated; in the LM's case, this was five-litres, and even with the supercharger's equivalence co-efficient applied, the 3.3-litre engine still came out as nominally below 5-litres.

Piper obtained the necessary supercharger, which was to be belt-driven from the front of the engine, and set about collecting the necessary parts, such as special low-compression pistons. Then came Le Mans 1967, and in its wake the CSI's controversial decision which altered so profoundly the whole face of sports-car racing. The supercharged 250LM would not have fitted into any category under the new regulations, and so, reluctantly, the project was shelved. The CSI had much to answer for.

So it was that the LM which Piper brought to Le Mans in 1968 was much closer to factory specification than it might have been. However, there were still quite a few ways in which it differed from the norm, the most obvious ones being in respect to bodywork.

A feature of most of Piper's cars is detachable front bodywork. Mid-engined Ferraris of the Sixties had fixed front bodywork, with a lift-out panel in the centre of the nose, to give access to fluid reservoirs, etc. The removable nose was intended especially for Le Mans, mainly in case of accident, as it is obviously much more convenient to remove and replace a piece of savaged bodywork than it is to try to repair it in situ. Apart from that advantage, the new, fibreglass, panel was both smoother and lighter than the aluminium original, and did away with the subframes needed for the lift-out panel. Fibreglass was chosen for the material because it is easier and cheaper to work with, and new panels can be made much faster. The tail and doors were also in fibreglass, all this being possible because the LM had been homologated with fibreglass specified as one of the bodywork materials.

The Piper 250LM was fitted with the standard Le Mans gear set, being of two available (the other, the Targa Florio set, had four close, low, ratios plus a long fifth designed for the Piccolo Madonie's long straight). Ratios and CWPs were rarely changed on LMs, as it was usually considered sufficient for the drop gears, at the back of the gearbox, to be changed to suit the requirements of a particular circuit.

When the LM was originally homologated, it had Dunlop solid-disc brakes, and the homologation was never updated to allow the use of ventilated discs (this again shows Ferrari's lack of interest in the car), so in the area of braking the car was always at a disadvantage compared with its newer rivals.

Preparing a car for Le Mans has changed a lot in the last twenty years, and the basic approach is now the exact opposite of what it used to be. While nowadays a car will be totally stripped and rebuilt, often with brand-new parts, between the final practice session and the race, in 1968 the policy was that if it ran all right in practice, it didn't get touched. One thing which has not changed is the building in of safety factors. Piper's 250LM had taps on the fuel pressure lines, so that if the gauge leaked it could be turned off. There was extra back-up in the shape of additional petrol pumps, a second battery, and switches so that changes from one to the other could be made, to allow a sick car to limp back to the pits.

At the back of the car, an additional pair of rear-lights was installed. These were fitted at the lower edge of the bodywork, tucked well under and forward of the rearmost part, to give them extra protection in the event of a rear-end shunt. A reserve fuel system was a must, and had to contain at least fuel for one complete lap of the 8.5-mile circuit. Also carried on board were a shovel and some stout netting, to enable a bogged-down car to be extricated from the sand at

Conventional mid Sixties rear suspension with compact fabricated upright - the 275LM was a no-nonsense car that a privateer could run without logistical problems.

Mulsanne corner; a complete tool kit was carried, plus assorted bits of tubing, wire and so on, together with a spare wheel, jack and wheelbrace.

Piper's LM had received a total engine rebuild prior to the Le Mans race. CSI regulations demanded that most parts of the engine be inspected by them to confirm their compliance with the rules of the day, then be stamped before being incorporated into the engine; pistons, heads, rods, all had to be officially stamped when the engine was being assembled at the factory. The motor was in superb condition, and gave all the power that was expected of it. Then, in practice, the dramas began.

During the first night's practice sessions Piper was motoring flat out down the Mulsanne straight when suddenly the engine note changed. He immediately slowed, and brought the LM into the pits for the situation to be investigated. The problem lay with one of the screws which held the trumpet on top of the front carburettor; nowadays the car has them drilled and wired up, but that was not the case back in 1968. The screw had come out, dropped down into the inlet tract, been sucked in to the engine, then got itself punched up into the cylinder head. There was no alternative but to return to base, about 20km from the circuit, pull the head off, clean up the piston and the combustion chamber and then put the whole thing back together again. It was a great pity that happened, because disturbing the engine which had proven so sweet undoubtedly took the edge off it.

At least, the engine trouble did not recur during the race, which was held in the damp, misty, chilly conditions of late September. The only significant problem which arose was electrical, and concerned the voltage regulators. The car been fitted with transistorised Prestolite voltage regulators, and it is thought that the diodes must have failed. Whatever the exact cause of the problem, the symptoms were clear enough: the 45ampere-hour alternator was boiling the water out of the battery and causing it to distort. Fortunately, it was at least still charging, for had it failed to do that then the car would undoubtedly have been forced to retire. Regulations forbade the battery being changed, so something had to be done to protect the two batteries carried on the car.

There wasn't the time to keep stopping to add distilled water, so a solution had to be found which would permit the car to continue with the minimum number of stops. Consequently, as dawn broke and cars' lights began to be switched off, the old LM was still circulating happily, quartz-halogen lights ablaze, these absorbing as much as possible of the excess current. Because the car had two batteries, the drivers kept on switching from one battery to the other, using a gas-filled changeover switch which allows this to be done whilst the batteries are in use, without blowing the diodes in the alternator.

Apart from the electrical problem, the car ran sweetly, and gave no other cause for concern. The weather was so wet that year that towards the end of the race the instruments were like fishbowls; the fuel pressure gauge, the fuel level gauge and the oil temperaturer gauge actually filled up with water, which the drivers could see swilling around inside the gauges!

Piper's 250LM was the only one of its type to finish at Le Mans in 1968, doing so in seventh place overall, second in Group Four to the winning Gulf Ford GT40. Apart from the remarkable result in 1965, it was the type's best placing at Le Mans.

Factory fresh, a 250LM sits in the workshops of British importer Maranaello Concessionaires. Note the regulation spare wheel at the back of this mid sixties customer sports-prototype.

FERRARI P2

In reaction to the serious challenge that Ford was making to its dominance of Prototype racing, Ferrari produced a completely new car for the 1965 season. The chassis was of the familiar multi-tubular spaceframe configuration but following the contemporary Formula One practice aluminium panels were added to certain tubes to provide stiffening. The suspension also reflected Grand Prix influence in the use of lower wishbones, single top links and radius arms at the rear. The traditional Borrani wire wheels were abandoned, replaced with cast magnesium rims of eight inch width at the front and nine inch at the rear enabling the use of Dunlop's latest specification tubeless tyres.

The bodywork, wind tunnel developed by Ferrari's own designers, featured a long low nose with a wide slot for the front mounted radiator. The mid section of the car was correspondingly low, accentuating the wheel arches that carried large air intakes at the rear. The general low line of the body necessitated a streamlined hump in the tail section to accommodate the carburettor stacks beneath the aerodynamic roll bar retained from the 275P.

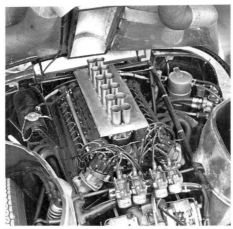

A completely new four cam engine was produced for works team's exclusive use in 3285cc (77 x 58.8mm) and 3987cc (77 x 71mm) form, both using twin plug, dual distributor ignition. Claimed outputs were 350 bhp at 8500 rpm for the 3.3 litre and 400 bhp at 8000 rpm for the 4.0 litre. For customer use the old twin cam engine was enlarged to 4390 cc (81 x 71 mm) producing 390 bhp at 7200 rpm. Thus, the chassis ran as a 275 P2 with the 4.4 engine.

For the 1965 Le Mans race a single coupe version was prepared running with a sloping rear window in practice that was removed before the race. Running in a works team comprising itself and two spyder-bodied 330 P2s the coupe retired from second place with seven hours left to run, its engine damaged by over revving.

In 1966 a single P2 was entered by the North American Racing Team with a new long tail coupe body design by Drogo along with three P2 customer cars which had been updated with body parts from the new P3 model and became, in factory parlance, 365Ps although to most people they were known as P2/3s. The P2 coupe driven by Gregory/Bondurant was retired after eight hours with gearbox problems while the P2/3s retired with a variety of engine and transmission problems.

The NART P2 returned again in 1967 to be driven by Pearson and Riccardo Rodriguez (no relation). They were the first Ferrari retirement when the latter planted it in the sandpit at the end of the straight where, despite the Mexican's digging, it remained.

FERRARI	
P2 - 1965	60 degree V12
Alloy plated spaceframe	4.0 litres
Suspension:	Alloy block
wishbone front	Carburettor
wishbone rear	24 valves
Engine semi-stressed	d.o.h.c.
Ferrari gearbox	Unblown
Flat bottom	400 b.h.p.

FERRARI 330 P3

Taking advantage of regulation changes with regard to the size of windscreens, the 1966 Ferrari P3 was lower and, due to the use of 8.5 inch wide front, 9.5 inch rear, wheels and a 2.5 inch broader track was wider than its P2 predecessor. The body shape designed by Modena stylist Piero Drogo was, as usual, beaten in aluminium, through for the first time some glassfibre panels were incorporated. The chassis was similar to that of the P2 in its use of an aluminium sheet reinforced tube frame while the suspension was altered only to accommodate wider tyres. A ZF five speed transmission replaced the P2's Ferrari gearbox. The engine was as used in the 330P2 but the use of Lucas fuel injection in place of the hitherto universal Weber carburettors increased power to 420 bhp at 8000 rpm with compression at 11.4:1. The wheelbase remained as per the P2.

Concentration on the new 3.0 litre Formula One had an adverse effect on the Ferrari prototype programme in 1966, a single car (if any) being run in the early season rounds of the Manufacturers Championship. At Le Mans three P3s were entered; two coupes run by the factory team plus a spyder entrusted to the North American Racing Team. The works car of Parkes and Scarfiotti was eliminated when the Italian collided with a spinning car in the dark while transmission failures saw to Bandini/Guichet and the NART car of Rodriguez/Ginther.

For the 1967 the P3s were handed on to favoured private teams after suspension modifications to allow wider wheels of the classic Campagnolo five spoke design. P4 type bodywork was also included in the up-rating, along with the fitting of the larger engine from the P2. The resulting car was known to the factory as the 412P but most remember it as the P3/4.

Three examples were entered at Le Mans, by the British Maranello Concessionnaires team (Attwood/Courage), NART (Rodriguez/Baghetti) and Scuderia Fillipinetti (Guichet/Miller).

The NART car ran as high as fourth in the opening laps of the race but eventually went out with an overheated engine. The Maranello car was sidelined by an oil pump failure while Fillipinetti's car went out with engine problems resulting from an oil leak.

FERRARI	
P3 - 1966	60 degree V12
Alloy plated spaceframe	4.0 litres
Suspension:	Alloy block
wishbone front	Fuel injected
wishbone rear	24 valves
Engine semi-stressed	d.o.h.c.
ZF gearbox	Unblown
Flat bottom	420 b.h.p.

FERRARI 330 P4

Having been beaten at Le Mans for the first time in seven years in 1966, Ferrari came back at Ford with the P4, an improved version of the P3. Three valve cylinder heads and a revised fuel injection system increased power to 450 bhp at 8000 rpm. The P3's ZF gearbox was replaced by a new Ferrari five speed design and rear disc brakes were hub mounted inside 11.5 inch wide Campagnolo wheels with 9.5 inch rims at the front. The chassis was much as that of its predecessor but with a lightly widened front track. Firestone tyres were used in preference to Dunlop and the whole machine was clothed in a subtly modified version of the P3 body. The extra width seemed to balance the car proportionately, making it one of the most attractive sports racing cars of its era.

That it was also fast and reliable was proved by early season wins at Daytona, on Ford territory, and, at home, at Monza. Four cars were entered for the 1967 Le Mans race three works cars plus a fourth given into the care of Equipe Nationale Belge. Parkes/Scarfiotti were quickest of the Ferrari contingent behind five Fords and a Chaparral. The British-Italian driver pairing finished an honourable second in the race having chased the winning Ford very hard all the way.

The Klass/Suttcliffe P4 was running third behind its team leader when the fuel injection pump failed in the 18th hour. Amon/Vaccarella were an early retirement when their car caught fire while the New Zealander was nursing it back to the pits on a rear wheel rim after a puncture. The loaned Belgian car of Mairesse/"Beurlys" repaid the faith shown in them by netting third place.

New regulations for 1968 restricted prototype engines to three litres so at the end of the 1967 the Ferrari P4's career, and indeed the big capacity P series lineage, came to an end. Two P4 chassis were converted for Can Am racing but met with negligible success.

FERRARI	
P4 - 1967	60 degree V12
Alloy plated spaceframe	4.0 litres
Suspension:	Alloy block
wishbone front	Fuel injected
wishbone rear	36 valves
Engine semi-stressed	d.o.h.c.
Ferrari gearbox	Unblown
Flat bottom	450 b.h.p.

EXPERIENCE COUNTS

Ferrari shrugged off Ford's massive Le Mans bid in '64 and '65 in spite of operating on a significantly smaller budget: experience was its wealth. By 1966 Ford had banked sufficient experience through its win at all costs policy. But Ferrari didn't give up and, as John Allen explains, even came back in 1967 with the beautiful P4.

In some ways the Ferrari 330P4 represented the end of an era. It first saw the light of day in 1967, yet it was a direct development of one of the earliest mid-engined sports cars, the 1963 Ferrari 250P, and it was essentially an outdated vehicle which was having to pit itself against much more modern opposition. That it fared as well as it did was more a tribute to the years of experience which Ferrari had amassed, than to any fundamental attributes of the car itself.

Ferrari approached the 1967 season with nothing really new in its armoury. Ford, on the other hand, was in the process of going ultra-modern with its aluminium honeycomb monocoque J-car/Mark IV, Chaparral was dabbling with the advanced technology of wings and automatic transmissions, and Lola was about to unveil its sports-racing version of the previously Group Seven-only T70, another aluminium monocoque. Ferrari's answer to the new wave challenge was to update the existing 330P3, and rechristen it 330P4.

In its principal form, as a Group Six sports-prototype, the 330P4 had only one season in which to prove itself, for like so many other cars it fell victim to the CSI axe which cut it down at the close of 1967. During that year the Ferrari works team raced the 330P4 at only six circuits, these being Daytona, Monza, Spa, the Targa Florio, Le Mans and Brands Hatch; two victories were obtained, at Daytona and Monza, but the important race, Le Mans, fell to the Ford

Mark IV, which took two wins from the only two races entered. Nevertheless, the 330P4's fine showing throughout the season was good enough (just) to hand the Sports Car Championship to Ferrari, which beat Porsche by 34 points to 32.

Usually referred to by the abbreviated version of its name, the P4 had descended from the 250P by way of the 275P and 330P of 1964, the 275P2 and 330P2 1965, and the 330P3 of 1966. It used the same basic method of construction - a steel tubular chassis - although on P3 and P4 this was stiffened by the addition of aluminium panels, in addition to the fibreglass ones as used on earlier cars. The P3 and P4 chassis were substantially lighter than that of the P2 (perhaps by as much as a third) thanks to the use of lighter-gauge tubing. Suspension of the P3 and P4 was also similar to that of the P2, which was the first Ferrari to use the then modern Formula One type, including trailing arms, but again the P3 and P4 benefitted from the use of lighter components. Shock-absorbers on the P3 were of steel, and non-adjustable, but those of the P4 were both lighter (aluminium) and also adjustable.

The most dramatic changes which occurred during the P4's evolution from the 250P were those of shape, for the mid-Sixties saw the start of a revolution in aerodynamics. Thanks to rule changes, and the 1966 introduction of a revised Appendix J which permitted sports cars to have narrower cockpits than previously, the P4, and the visually almost identical P3, become

The P4 essentially followed the shape of the Drogo-bodied P3, but featured this wrap-around rear spoiler. 1967 was the year of the Chaparral high wing car.

significantly slimmer and sleeker than their immediate ancestors; even so, it appears that none of these cars had the right shape to go really fast.

One of the most revealing sources of aerodynamic information is the Le Mans speed trap, a radar system which sits at the side of the Mulsanne Straight and tells the truth - or at least, as close to the truth as anyone is likely to get - about which is the fastest of them all. Conditions change from year to year, as does the radar, but for any given year comparisons between cars ought to be valid. The P4 does not emerge well from the data obtained at Le Mans in 1967: the three works P4s, each with some 450bhp on tap, recorded maxima of 192.6, 189.5 and 192.6 mph, whilst a fourth P4, nominally an Equipe Nationale Belge entry, was measured at 192.0mph; the average of the maxima for the four cars comes out at 191.7mph. Ford's works Mark IVs, the chief adversaries of the Ferraris, presented much more respectable figures, ranging from 206.9mph. The advantage of nearly nineteen miles per hour could not all be due to the Fords' greater power (reputedly 500bhp), but was also the result of a much better shape.

Differences between the shapes of the Drogo-bodied P3 and the P4 relate to details only. For example, the pedal box on the P3, which had intruded into the radiator air outlet on that model, was reversed on the P4, allowing the air outlet to be larger front-to-back, and so aid airflow. At the extreme front of the car, the lower headlights were raised slightly and positioned a little further forward, allowing more space for canard fins to be fitted. At the back, the P4 featured a full width spoiler as on the P3, but with extensions which wrapped around to the sides of the car. Both fixed-head coupe and open spyder bodywork was available, the two styles being interchangeable, with the open version (lighter by some 40kg) favoured for slow circuits where aerodynamics were of lesser importance.

Just as the P4's shape differed only slightly from that of the P3, the changes under the skin were relatively minor, with one exception. Whilst the P3 had two valves per cylinder, the heads of the P4 were endowed with three per cylinder, one exhaust and two inlet. The revised valve layout necessitated modifications to the tuned exhaust system to suit the changed characteristics of the classic V12, and experiments were carried out with balance pipes which linked the cylinders on the two sides of the engine.

The P4 made use of the same basic engine design as its predecessors, although the 250P of 1963 and the 330P4 of 1967 had virtually no parts in common. The overall capacity of the dry-sump 4-cam V12 remained unchanged from the P3 at 3967cc (77mm bore and 71mm stroke), but

the claimed power output was up by some 30bhp. Lucas fuel injection was fitted, as on the P3, but at the same time Ferrari produced a carburetted version of the old two-valve engine, for use in a customer-car version of the P4, these being converted P3s, renamed as 412Ps (although at the time everyone called them 330P3/4s). The engine of the P4 was used as a partially-stressed part of the structure, but the positions of the twelve mounting points differed slightly from those on the 412P; thus, a P4 engine cannot be dropped into a 412P without there being modifications made to the chassis of the latter.

Other mechanical improvements over the P3 were equally small. The wheels, which on the P3 had been Dunlop light alloys with small rectangular holes, were replaced by Campagnolo magnesium castings with a five-pointed star design. These were wider than before, with the result that the rear wheels (at 11.5 inches up by two inches over those of the P3) in particular were deeply dished, requiring knock-off spinners with ears angled well out from the wheel centres. Tyres were Firestone, replacing the Dunlops which had previously been used by works Ferraris.

The Girling brakes, with four-pot calipers, were outboard, unlike the three-pot brakes on early P3s, this making disc-changes easier; here, Ferrari was learning from Ford. During 1966 Maranello had been developing its own new gearbox, capable of accepting the torque of the 4-litre engine, but this was not ready in time for the P3, which had instead been fitted with a 5DS25, a proprietory 'box by ZF. By the end of 1966 the new five-speed synchromesh Ferrari gearbox was ready, and was fitted into the P4. As was standard practice for Ferrari, two gear sets were available, a "Targa-Florio" group with four low ratios plus a high fifth, and a normal set, with all five ratios being fairly evenly spaced.

A useful improvement to the cooling system was the incorporation of a valve which shut off the header tank from the rest of the system; this permitted water to be added to

the header tank even when the engine was hot, removing the risk of the pressurised system blowing hot water out as soon as the pressure cap was released. The engine oil-cooler was an unusual device, an expensive coiled and finned tube nicknamed serpente and installed behind the water radiator.

Fuel was housed in twin bag-tanks, one on each side of the car, and containing a total of 140 litres. A cross-over tube (actually part of the chassis structure) linked the two tanks, and enabled both to be filled from either of the two fillers, and also allowed fuel to be drawn off from both tanks without the need to switch from one to the other. Racing in wet weather brought to light problems with windscreen wiper motors, the original Lucas units used by the first P4s and 412Ps falling during the downpour at Spa, in 1967; as a result, the Lucas motors were replaced with Marelli units.

After its career as a contender in the Sports Car Championship ended, the P4 was adapted as a Can-Am car, two examples of the type being cut down to spyder configuration, with low-height windscreen, engine enlarged to 4.2-litres, and with revised aerodynamics both at front and rear. The cars were too heavy and too underpowered to provide any serious opposition to existing dedicated Can-Am cars, and they failed to shine in their new role. The original tube-frame P-series was at the limit of its development by the end of the 1967 season, and it is interesting to note that when Ferrari rejoined sports-car racing, at the beginning of 1969, the car which it used still featured a tube-frame chassis, but with so much reinforcement by stressed alloy skinning that it was virtually a semi - monocoque.

Start of the 1967 race: Ford already ahead. The works Ferrari P4s are evident some way down the starting line, including car 24 (behind Ford MkIV number 1). This was an unequal struggle yet Ferrari gave its all.

FERRARI 312P

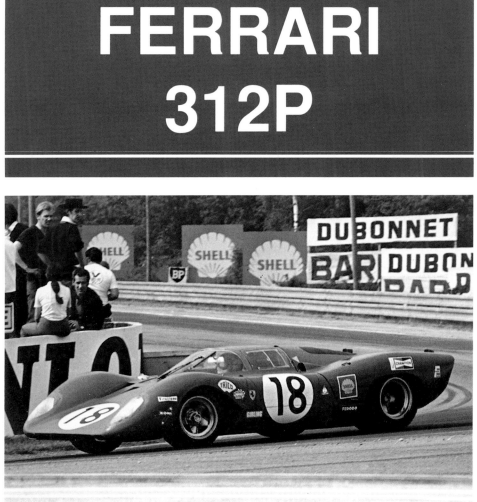

Ferrari shunned the Manufacturers Championship in 1968 in an effort to improve its single seater fortunes. However, 1969 saw a 3.0 litre V12 prototype make its debut at Sebring. The engine was that of the current Formula One car, a four valve per cylinder four cam 60 degree V12 with Lucas fuel injection and a claimed output of 430 bhp at 9800 r.p.m. The transmission was a five speed Ferrari design with a twin plate clutch. On its debut inboard rear brakes were fitted but these were later moved to an outboard position. The bodywork was in glassfibre with an open top similar to that of the 1968 612P CanAm car, with a snorkel type air collector box behind the driver's left shoulder ram feeding air to the twelve inlet stacks. Running in this guise the 312P contested most of the early season races with second places on its debut and at Spa the best results against heavy works Porsche opposition.

In preparation for Le Mans two chassis were fitted with coupe roof sections and stronger gearboxes. Qualified 6th and 7th by Rodriguez/Piper and Amon/Schetty, the latter car became involved in Woolfes' fatal accident at Maison Blanche on the first lap. Amon struck the crashed cars' detached

and burning fuel tank which engulfed his Ferari in flames from which he was fortunate to escape unscathed. Rodriguez/ Piper lasted until the 14th hour when a gearbox problem ended their race.

The 312P coupes were purchased by NART and one returned to Le Mans in 1970 to be driven by Posey/Adamowicz. An accident in the rain and engine troubles meant that, although the car was still running after 24 hours, insufficient distance had been covered for it to be classified as a finisher. Surprisingly, in 1974 one of the 312Ps returned to Le Mans, albeit rebodied with spyder coachwork of a more modern design, and finished in ninth place.

FERRARI	
312P - 1969	60 degree V12
Alloy plated spaceframe	3.0 litres
Suspension:	Alloy block
wishbone front	Fuel injected
wishbone rear	48 valves
Engine semi-stressed	d.o.h.c.
Ferrari gearbox	Unblown
Flat bottom	430 b.h.p.

FERRARI 512S

Fiat's acquisition of a 50% stake in Ferrari in June 1969 resulted in the budget being made available to produce a batch of twenty five Group Five sportscars, providing a serious challenger to the Porsche 917. The Ferrari 512S was designed and built by a team led by Mauro Forghieri, in less than five months. The engine was derived from an earlier Can Am power unit and was a 60 dry sump, water cooled V12 with bore and stroke of 87 x 70 mm, displacing 4993.5 ccm. The alloy block had cast iron wet liners and the alloy heads were of double overhead camshaft configuration. With Marelli Dinoplex ignition and Lucas fuel injection power was claimed as 550 bhp at 8000 rpm.

The chassis was a tubular steel spaceframe with stressed alloy panelling around the cockpit area. Fuel was carried in bag tanks fitted in the side sponsons. The engine was carried as a semi stressed member. Twin water radiators were mounted on either wide of the cockpit forewall drawing air through door ducts. Bodywork saw glassfibre nose and tail panels attached directly to the alloy panelled central section. Girling disc brakes were hub mounted and had single calipers and Ferodo pads. Transimission was by an AP triple plate clutch, ZF limited slip differential and Ferrari's own five speed gearbox.

The factory entered four longtails which were backed up by seven "reinforcements"; two Scuderia Fillipinetti cars, a NART chassis and an Ecurie Francorchamps 512s in longtail form, plus three short tail cars; a Fillipnetti coupe, a similar Gelo car and an Escuderia Montjuich machiune which was the only one to run in spyder form.

Practice indicated that the race held the prospect of being a classis Le Mans encournter between a manufacturer seeking to re-establish itself and an other desperately trying to win for the first time. When the fastest works car of Vaccarella, second behind a streamlined Porsche 912 in qualifying, retired with a broken connecting rod, in the first hour things looked gloomy.

Much worse was to follow. Heavy rain began during the second hour and continued as a convoy of four 512s came up to lap one of the works Alfa Romeos at the tight Indianapolis corner.

The Alfa swerved to avoid a slower car and in an instant there were Ferraris spinning and crashing all over the track. Wisell in a Fillipinetti long tail car hit the Alfa and was collected by Regazzoni in a works car. Parkes'second Fillipinetti long tail also made solid contact and momentarily caught fire. Somehow the Englishman got the car back to the pits but it was too badly damaged to continue. Bell in another works car had managed to miss everyonebut over revved the engine and wwas also out of the race.

At quarter distance Ickx/Schetty had the surviving works car running in third place which later became second when the leading Porsche encountered difficulties just after midnight. Less than two hours later, however, Ickx crashed at the Ford chicane, killing an unfortunate track marshal, when he hit a puddle at high speed. The car caught fire vbut the driver escaped unharmed. The short tail Fillipinetti car was next to go out with a broken half short after a spin. The Gelo car having long since been withdrawn wityh handling problems, only two from the eleven starters made it to the finish, the Posey/Bucknum NART car, running only eleven cylinders for the last eight hours, finished fourth while the yellow Belgian car was firth having suffered fuel feed problems.

FERRARI	
512S - 1970	60 degree V12
Alloy plated spaceframe	5.0 litres
Suspension:	Alloy block
wishbone front	Fuel injected
wishbone rear	48 valves
Engine semi-stressed	d.o.h.c.
Ferrari gearbox	Unblown
Flat bottom	550 b.h.p.

FERRARI 512M/F

By the time of the 1971 race the five litre Ferrari had been upgraded to 512M specification. An inttensive programme of revisions masterminded by Biacomo Caliri gave rise to a new body shape on which only the windscreen and roof were retained from the 512s. A new wedge shaped nose carried a single oil cooler while the mid section had lower radiator air ducts ahead of a flatter rear deck which was reminiscent of the rival Porsche 917. An air collector scoop was fitted to the injection stacks with small twin aerofoils mounted either side of the central rear spoiler. The engine had received further attention and an output of 616bhp had been achieved. By this time, however, the works team was concentrating all effort on the development of a new 3.0 litre prototype in preparation for the new rules coming into effect for 1972.

Works preparation for the 1971 race was available at a price and most of the European private entrants considered it money well spent. However, of the nine car Ferrari Group 5 entry the fastest in qualifying was the NART entered. Roger Penske prepared 512M. The car had been completely stripped down and rebuilt by the American team incorporating many improvements including a new refuelling system, revised springing, a full width rear aerofoil and revisions to the brakes to make pad changes faster and easier. The engine had been modified by Traco Engineering with new valves and springs and improved power was claimed at around 600 bhp.

The Penske car was certainly quick, qualifying fourth behind the longtail Porsches. Scuderia Fillipinetti had also decided to go its own way and produced a chassis dubbed the 512F which featured a full width rear wing similar to that of Penske. However, the aerodynamic changes carried out by Mike Parkes and his team also included the narrowing of the cockpit and the lowering of the windscreen which improved radiator cooling and air penetration. A larger than standard air scoop was also fitted. Parkes qualified eighth behind Vaccarellia in the Montjuich 512M that the Sicillian was

sharing with Juncadella. The Penske car confirmed its practice form by leading the Ferrari challenge until its engine broke in the fifth hour. The 512F lasted until 1am when, after Parkes damaged the car in a spin at Maison Blanche, it was repaired and returned to the race only to retire after a few laps with no oil presure.

Some of the standard 512Ms enjoyed better fortune. However, the Vaccarella/Junacadella car had run strongly enough to lead the race at half distance only for the gearbox to break minutes later. The NART car of Posey/Adamowicz finished third while Craft and Weir in the latter's 512M were fourth, eleven laps behind at the finish. Of the others, the Loos/Pesch Gelo car broke a piston while the Manfredini/Gagliardi Fillipinetti car and the de Cadenet/de Fierlant Francorchamps car both suffered gearbox failures. The only 512s in the race, entered by NART for Gregory/Eaton, was eliminated early on by fuel feed difficulties.

A change of regulations at the end of the 1971 season ended the international racing career of the Ferrari 512 and with it one of the classic eras of sportscar racing.

FERRARI	
512M - 1971	60 degree V12
Alloy plated spaceframe	5.0 litres
Suspension:	Alloy block
wishbone front	Fuel injected
wishbone rear	48 valves
Engine semi-stressed	d.o.h.c.
Ferrari gearbox	Unblown
Flat bottom	600b.h.p.

FORD GT40
ALLOY BLOCK

In February 1963 negotiations for the purchase of Ferrari broke down and as a direct result Ford of America decided to build its own sports-racing car with which to contest the Le Mans 24 Hour race. A subsidiary operating under the name of Ford Advanced Vehicles was established at Slough in the south east of England under the direction of Roy Lunn, John Wyer and Eric Broadley. The latter had produced, in late 1962, a mid engined coupe powered by the same engine Ford was intending to use in its prototype. The two existing Lola GTs were purchased by FAV and became mobile test beds for components for the emerging Ford Prototype. During initial design studies, completed in May 1963, an overall height of 40 inches was arrived at; thus the car became known as the GT40.

The finished chassis was a mid engined coupe based around a fabricated sheet steel monocoque which gave strength and rigidity for an enormous weight penalty. Rubber sealed box section sills formed the fuel tanks and a forward structure carried the front mounted water and oil radiator. Suspension was by double wishbones and coil spring/dampers. The sills were extended rearwards beyond the firewall to form sponsons on which was mounted the rear suspension; trailing arms, single top links and lower wishbones and coil spring/dampers.

Transmission was via a four speed Colotti gearbox and a three plate Borg and Beck clutch while the engine was a 90 degree pushrod V8 based on the Fairlane production engine which was also being developed as an Indianapolis unit. Displacing 4195cc it produced 350 bhp at 7200rpm on four twin choke Weber carburettors. Borrani fifteen inch wide wire wheels were fitted to aid the cooling of the outboard 11.5 inch Girling disc brakes.

The bodywork, evolved via wind tunnel tests in America, featured a blunt rounded nose with air directed through a front aperture by an air dam which also collected air for a complex cockpit and engine bay cooling system. Deep door cutaways in the roof enabled easy access to the cockpit. The rear bodywork ventilated the engine and rear brakes by scoops on the trailing edges of the doors.

In mid-April, just two months after the final drawings were completed, a pair of cars was sent to the Le Mans test weekend and both were damaged in accidents resulting from a high speed aerodynamic imbalance. The problem was solved in subsequent testing by the fitting of a spoiler across the tail. Three cars were entered in June. Further revisions were evident for the race, including the cutting of additional cooling apertures in the nose and the widening of the front air dam to balance the rear spoiler.

Ginther/Gregory led during the early laps but retired after four and a half hours when the gearbox failed. Attwood/Schlesser exited in flames when a fuel line fractured while Phil Hill/McLaren spent most of the first hour dashing in and out of the pits for attention to minor problems but managed to work their way up to fourth place during the night before they, too, suffered a gearbox failure. A small consolation for the team was a new lap record by Hill.

FORD	
GT40 - 1964	90 degree V8
Steel monocoque	4.2 litres
Suspension:	Alloy block
wishbone front	Carburettor
wishbone rear	16 valves
Engine unstressed	Pushrod
Colotti gearbox	Unblown
Flat bottom	350 b.h.p.

FORD GT40

IRON BLOCK

Returning to Le Mans in 1965, numerous changes had been made to the GT40. Shelby's Cobra version of the Fairlane engine was fitted, increasing power to 390 bhp at 7000rpm. The weight increase caused by use of Shelby's iron block 4736cc engine was offset by the removal of the nose mounted oil tank, no longer required by the wet sump unit. The Colotti gearbox received Ford internals for early season races but by Le Mans had been replaced by a five speed ZF transmission. Aerodynamics had also come under scrutiny, tests having revealed that inefficient internal airflow was sapping power by more than 70 bhp.

The original cockpit cooling system was abandoned in favour of bodywork surface ducting. Brake cooling problems were addressed by the fitting of Hallibrand cast magnesium wheels which incorporated vanes that blew air onto the disc through centrifugal force.

The main works effort for the 1965 race was belatedly channelled into the 7.0 litre MkII project, with four MkIs entered as back ups by private teams. The two Shelby MkIs originally to have been run by the factory were entrusted to Rob Walker and Scuderia Fillipinetti, running alongside an F.A.V. chassis and a Ford France car. In what works driver Ken Miles called "the greatest defeat ever suffered by a team in the history of motor racing", all six Fords, despite playing leading roles in the race, had retired by midnight. Another lap record by a MkII was scant reward for the effort.

By the time of the 1966 race, the MkI GT40 had been homologated as a Group 4 car and was still strictly the domain of private entrants. Five appeared for various teams to be raced by drivers of the calibre of Rindt, Ickx, Revson and Ireland. Yet again none were to finish, the last retiring when fuel leaked onto a rear tyre and caused it to spin.

In 1967 three MkIs ran and again none made the finish, one car making a fiery departure at Mulsanne corner. At the Le Mans test weekend a chassis modified by J.W. Automotive, the company formed by John Wyer and John Willment after the former's departure from Ford Advanced Vehicles had appeared, entered as a Mirage. The lower portion of the chassis was standard GT40 with the upper section reshaped to a design by Len Bailey with a narrower roof area and sloping door windows aiming for a reduction in drag. Initially the Mirage ran with the regular 4.7 litre V8 engine but by Le Mans both team cars were fitted with 5.7 litre Holman and Moody units. The cars qualified 15th and 16th but both were among the early retirements with engine problems, Ickx/Muir lasting but three hours, Piper/Thompson barely an hour longer.

For 1968 J.W. Automotive converted one of the cars it had run as a Mirage back to standard configuration and ran it alongside two other GT40s in a season long battle with the works Porsche team culminating at Le Mans.

Rodriguez/Bianchi saw a strong Zuffenhausen challenge evaporate before quarter-distance, moving into a lead they were never to lose. Things were less straightforward for their team mates; one car was buried deeply in the Mulsanne Corner sandtrap, taking no further part, the other suffered terminal engine failure. Two more, privately entered cars also failed to finish.

By 1969 the GT40 design was entering its sixth year of competition and was looking distinctly unsophisticated in comparison to some of its rivals. J.W.A. ran its own Mirage-B.R.M. 3.0 litre prototype in early races with disappointing results, so the faithful GT40 was re-enlisted for Le Mans. In the closest finish in the history of the race, Jacky Ickx, co-driven by Jackie Oliver, beat the works Porsche of Herrmann/Larrousse by just 100 metres. J.W.A.'s second car finished third while a German entered GT40 was sixth. Of the two other GT40 entries, one retired with alternator problems, the other was withdrawn having fallen far behind after major repairs in the pits.

METAMORPHOSIS

Ironically, it was Ford's withdrawal from international sports car racing that gave JW Automotive the possibility to make a winner out of the hitherto unsuccessful Ford GT40. Superb preperation was a vital aspect of the crack team's winning formula. GT40 historian John Allen discussed it with contemporary JW Automotive mechanic Alan Hearn.

If a prize had ever been offered for the most improved sports-racing car, then the 1968 Gulf Ford GT40 would have been a strong contender to win it. It is surprising how much better that car was than its 1964 to 1967 antecedents; from an unreliable mid-field make-weight to an extremely quick and dependable long-distance runner took just one winter to achieve, and most of the credit for getting there can go to a combination of Gurney-Weslake cylinder heads and meticulous preparation.

JW Automotive Engineering, the John Wyer/John Willment-owned company which on 1 January 1967 had taken over the assets of Ford Advanced Vehicles Limited, stood both to win and to lose from the CSI's banning of large capacity prototypes at the end of 1967. On the debit side, the company's Mirage M1, which had been emerging as a force to be reckoned with, had been rendered obsolete by the rule-changes; the credit side of the balance was that the old GT40, long thought to be well past its prime, was ideally placed to profit from the changing situation.

One factor which contributed to the GT40's success, achieved so late in its life, was its rugged construction. It had always been excessively heavy, and whilst this had counted against it when it was taking on Ferrari, it acted in the car's favour when it was competing against new and unproven cars in 1968 and 1969. The sturdiness of the GT40 was not confined to its heavy steel monocoque chassis, for virtually all components had been over-engineered to a substantial degree, and after the original Colotti gearbox had been replaced with the tough ZF, it was extremely rare for a GT40 to retire because of failure of a chassis, suspension or driveline component. The Achilles-heel was the engine, for whilst this was generally reliable enough in sprint events - ie, those lasting around six hours - the inherent weaknesses in its road-car cylinder head gasket design, and in various other production components, generally made it too weak to last out the 24-hour grind at Le Mans.

After Ford withdrew its factory teams (Shelby American and Holman & Moody)

from official participation with the GT Marks II and IV, the company made available to JW Automotive some of the beefed-up engine parts which Ford had been developing, but which they had hitherto not released (the inference is that during 1967 they had no wish to see the works cars being humbled by a reliable Mirage). The engine modifications transformed the GT40's motor, and meant that, for the first time in its already long career, the small-block version of the car was both reliable enough and fast enough to take on the competition on equal terms.

The record of JW Automotive's two seasons with the GT40 is a tribute to the car's reliability. The Gulf-sponsored cars took part in a total of twelve races, and won seven of them; other finishes out of the 23 entries in those twelve races were one second, two thirds, one fourth, one fifth and one sixth. In 1968 the five wins achieved were sufficient to give Ford the championship by 45 points to Porsche's 42. The two seasons 1968 and 1969 had seen JW Automotive use only four GT40s in all, with only one event, Le Mans 1968, finding more than two of them fielded together; this makes its achievements all the more remarkable.

Having cars which were so sturdily built meant that JW's mechanics were probably not quite as over-worked as were those of some of its opponents. The GT40 had been very carefully designed with long-distance racing in mind, and as a result its general accessibility was good, and it posed little in the way of problems for the mechanics. One of the jobs which was really disliked, both for its difficulty and the time needed to complete it, was the replacement of the rubber fuel bag tanks. Two such tanks were fitted, one in each sill, and to replace them they had to be fed into the sill via an opening immediately behind each front wheel. The

Le Mans can be a trying race for a mechanic. Here, in 1968, Hearn and John Collins change the clutch on the Hobbs/Hawkins GT40. Note detached ZF gearbox.

problem concerned the interior of the sills, which were webbed for additional (and probably unnecessary) strength. Despite liberal coatings of french chalk, the fuel bags were prine to snag on each and every protusion, and getting them into place, then ensuring that the access panels in the tops of the sill, and the joints with the under-seat crossover tubes linking both tanks together, were fuel tight, was a long and tedious operation.

During the season, small quantities of fuel would inevitably leak into the sills, and sit there until the season's end, when the cars would be stripped and rebuilt. On one occasion the fuel remained undiscovered until welding operations started, when it declared its presence with explosive, but thankfully not dangerously so, results.

Another task which failed to find favour was the fitting of bodywork on newly built GT40s, this again being a time-consuming and boring operation. The fibreglass on GT40s was much thicker (and heavier) than on modern sports-racers, and straight from the mould it rarely fitted the car for which it was intended. The doors were especially difficult to fit, as not only did they have to match the side contours of the car, they also had to blend in with the roof, and fit snugly beneath metal "eyebrows" which held them in place. Windows, too, were a problem, as the plastic side-windows were prone to splitting as they were drilled to accept rivets; the glass windscreen, which was bonded into position, took an age to remove and refit, the required glue being so stiff that it was generally stirred by means of a power-drill fitted with a paddle.

Probably the most inaccessible parts on the GT40 were the attachment points for the radius arms, these being buried deep inside the monocoque. Fortunately, they rarely needed attention, and once the car had been assembled at the beginning of the season it was unlikely that the radius arms would need attention before the end. One component which never worried the mechanics was the ZF gearbox, simply because they never touched the inside of it. The ZF was a superb piece of machinery, very reliable and with synchromesh, nowadays a rare luxury on racing cars. The reason that the mechanics never touched it was that it was almost impossible for anyone other than a specialist to work on, and even a skilled ZF fitter would require a whole day to complete a change of ratios. For most races JW took with them extra gearboxes with different ratios fitted, so that the entire gearbox could be changed if a change of ratios was deemed necessary. The exception was Le Mans (different in just about every respect) when JW took with them Stan Litt, a ZF expert, just in case anything went wrong; it never did.

Working for JW Automotive certainly had its bright moments. One of these came

whenever the team visited Le Mans, and stayed, as usual, at the Hotel de France in La Chartre-sur-le-Loir. It was the task of the mechanics to drive the cars for which they were responsible the forty-five or so kilometres to the circuit. Driving the world's premier sports-racing cars (unlicensed, of course) on public roads was something which was eagerly looked forward to, and the GT40 was such a docile, tractable beast that it never gave any problems when used on the road. In 1969, following the epic Le Mans battle which saw the Ickx/Oliver GT40 triumph over the Herrmann/Larrousse Porsche 908, both the winning GT40 and its sister car, which came third, were entrusted to their respective mechan-

Yes, that is a dipstick! Hearn checks the oil level during qualifying at Le Mans

ics for the drive back to La Chartre. Unfortunately, they got lost on the way. By using back roads in order to miss the traffic, both cars were well and truly lost, and that Sunday evening many a sleepy Sarthe village rang to the sound of a pair of unmuffled V8s, as four happy mechanics and two healthy GT40s gradually wound their way South, and (eventually) found Gulf's HQ at La Chartre.

Pit stop for Hailwood's GT40 at Le Mans '69. Alan Hearn is working on the drivers side, Ray Jones opposite. Team Manager David Yorke (right) keeps an eye on proceedings.

FORD GT40 MKII

In the winter of 1964 a Ford GT40 was fitted with a 427 cubic inch Galaxie engine and the MkII was unintentionally born. The use of the large 7.0 litre power unit was purely experimental. With a NASCAR racing pedigree the V8 developed 485 bhp at 6200 cc displacement. The two valve push rod engine was known as "the wedge" on account of its combustion chamber shape and it was fitted into the chassis by moving forward the driving position and altering the rear bulkhead to accomodate its extra length. Wider cast magnesium Hallibrand wheels were fitted, as were (outboard mounted) disc brakes which were solid at the rear and ventilated at the front. Transmission was by Ford's own four speed T44 transaxle incorporating a self locking differential in conjunction with a Long twin plate clutch. The front structure of the car was extended forward to carry an enlarged water radiator, new front brake ducting and an oil tank for the engine. While the glassfibre bodywork enclosing the rear of the car was similar to that of the "MkI", the longer nose section had a tidier single opening for the radiator.

In practice for Le Mans the two Mark IIs sprouted a variety of fins and spoilers on the nose and tail in an effort to make the cars handle. Deletion of the rear anti-roll bar finally made for stability at speeds in excess of 200 mph. Despite the problems Phil Hill stunned the Ferrari opposition with a qualifying time over five seconds quicker than his nearest Maranello rival. In the race the MkIIs held station in first and second places in the opening hours before gearbox failures eliminated both cars. Hill had, however, set a new lap record and a new race speed record on the straight of 199mph.

Come the 1966 race, the MkII had a full season of competition development behind it. In late 1965 a shorter, lower nose, developed by Shelby, was tested showing an increase in stability and top speed and a reduction in weight. A new lighter tail section, and an improved engine were also introduced. February 1966 saw the Fords sweep the board at Daytona with four cars in the first five places. Ventilated rear brakes were adopted at Sebring (with extra cooling scoops) another 1-2 finish resulting. Meanwhile, 7.0 litre engines were being run on computer simulated laps of the Le Mans circuit for up to forty eight hours in preparation for the culmination of three years' endeavour. In Le Mans form the engine was now producing 485 bhp at 6300 rpm.

Eight Mk IIs were entered for the 1966 race, three Shelby cars, three for Holman and Moody and two for the British Alan Mann team. Gurney was fastest qualifier in a Shelby Mk II, seven seconds inside the lap record, heading a line of four Fords at the front of the starting echelon. After 12 hours of the race MkIIs filled the first four places; the Ferrari opposition appeared to be wilting.

Despite the lap speeds being reduced in the interest of reliability, by the end of the race only three cars were still running. However, they were in first, second and third places. In a bungled attempt at stage-managing a dead heat finish, the Hulme/Miles car that had led for so long was adjudged to have been beaten by the similar McLaren/Amon car that had started two places further back and had therefore covered a greater distance.

Three MkIIs appeared again in the 1967 race supporting the main factory effort with the MkIV. Hawkins' MkII led its illustrious high tech brothers early in the race until sidelined when its V8 dropped a valve. The other two cars were involved in an all-Ford multiple accident in the dark.

FORD	
Mk2 - 1965	90 degree V8
Steel monocoque	7.0 litres
Suspension:	Iron block
wishbone front	Carburettor
wishbone rear	16 valves
Engine unstressed	Pushrod
Ford gearbox	Unblown
Flat bottom	485 b.h.p.

THE LOST WINNER

Ford tried to buy Ferrari but failed. Then it tried to beat Ferrari at Le Mans in '64 but failed. It tried again in '65, only to fail again. Clearly its 1966 triumph was something rather special, the winning Mark 2 a motor car of great historical significance. Nevertheless, it got lost. Ronnie Spain helped find the GT40 P/1046. Here he tells its involved story.

At 4.00 pm on Saturday June 18 1966 a Ford GT40 Mark 2 - more particularly chassis number GT40 P/1046 - set off with 54 other cars to contest the 34th Le Mans 24 hour endurance race. 3009.35 miles later it led home two other Mark 2's in Ford's famous staged 1 - 2 - 3 finish.

This is the story of GT40 P/1046.

The 1966 Le Mans win was the culmination of over three years of concerted effort by the Ford Motor Company which had begun back in 1963 when the decision had been taken to involve the company in long distance sports car racing - with the ultimate goal being the publicity a win at Le Mans would bring. After an almost successful attempt to buy an interest in Ferrari failed in May, Ford realised there was no other way than to build its own car for the task. A team of designers under Roy Lunn, including Eric Broadley, Len Bailey and Phil Remington was drawn together - and the car they produced less than a year later was the Ford GT40. Although in the early days it was known simply as the Ford GT, the 40 soon became officially tagged on, it being a reference to the car's forty inch height in the initial design studies.

The car comprised a semi-monocoque chassis built from 024-029 inch sheet steel with square tube stiffening and a reinforced fibreglass body, with independent front and rear suspension - the front being double wishbone and the rear having upper and lower trailing arms with lower wishbone and transverse upper link. Powered initially by Ford's 256 cubic inch Indy engine with 4-speed Colotti transmissions, from the fifth chassis on the cars used 289 inch Cobra units matched with 5 speed ZF boxes.

The first car was completed on April 1 1964 (and destroyed at the Le Mans trials on April 18) and a team of three cars was ready - in theory - for Le Mans in June. But there had been insufficient time for testing,

especially of components, and the last of the three cars was out after only 13 1/2 hours.

While these three cars and others continued to test and race - unsuccessfully - for the rest of the season, the path which would eventually lead to 1046 winning Le Mans was already being trodden, for in July the go-ahead was given to build up two bare chassis already at Kar Kraft - a special performance unit set up by Ford in Detroit - to be powered by Ford's big 427 inch engine. The first of these cars GT/106 ran for the first time in mid-May, and second time out at Ford's Romeo Proving Ground it clocked 210 mph. It was decided to run it and its sister car GT/107 at Le Mans, by then only a month away. Not surprisingly, however, it proved to be a repeat of the previous year, as the two new cars entered by Los Angeles, California, based Shelby American Inc., were once again virtually untested (in fact in 107's case totally untested, prior to its arrival at the track) with 106 retiring in the fifth hour with a broken transmission and 107 - admittedly outlasting all the other GT40's in the race - retiring with a broken engine after only 6 hours 45 minutes.

Despite this dismal showing it was considered worth one more attack on Le Mans and by early August new bare chassis for completion as 427 powered cars, now officially to be known as Mark 2's, had begun to arrive in pairs from Slough in England, while the test programme recommenced with 106 and 107. And as the season progressed many improvements were implemented in the areas of transmission, brakes and cooling systems for the engine and transaxle. In addition, following the chassis breakage occurring at the lower front suspension pick up points of 106 while testing at Daytona in August (although this was chiefly felt to be as a result of it being one of a batch of four lighter gauge steel cars) the chassis of all

future Mark 2's would be reinforced in these heavily stressed areas.

Early December saw the completion of the first two new Mark 2's, GT40 P/1011 and 1012. The whole front of the new Mark 2 had been reworked and was now clothed in a body section basically of 1965 GT40 production type, widened and deepened to allow for the bigger tyres. On January 17 1966 the ranks of Mark 2's in the programme swelled to eight with the arrival at Shelby-American of GT40 P/1046 and 1047 as bare chassis on slave wheels and tyres.

By the time the Daytona 24 Hours came along in February the entry list included five of the new Mark 2's, two of which were entered by Holman and Moody, a new team recruited to the ranks. And at last things

started to go Ford's way with only one Mark 2 failing to finish and the others, headed by GT40 P/1015, coming home 1st, 2nd, 3rd and 5th.

This was followed by a 1st and 2nd at Sebring from a four car entry and even a 2nd at Spa with a single Mark 2 entry which was still running its Le Mans gears - it being the surviving car from the Le Mans Trials at which the other Mark 2 had been destroyed in Walt Hansgen's fatal accident.

And so - once again - to Le Mans. But this time, for the first time, with a line-up of eight cars built to a tried and tested configuration. 1046 along with 1015 and 1047 were entered by Shelby-American, 1016, 1031 and 1032 by Holman and Moody, and XGT-1 and XGT-2 by Alan Mann from England, with 1012 and XGT-3 as spares. 1046 had

flown to France on June 1 and had first run on May 22 back at Riverside in a one hour Le Mans shakedown. It was finished in black with twin white stripes and housed engine number AX-316-1-41.

When the eight Mark 2's took their places on the grid for the traditional Le Mans start on Saturday June 18 it was with 1046 fourth in line behind three other Mark 2's, with a qualifying time set by Bruce McLaren - co-driving with Chris Amon - of 1 m. 32.6 s., exactly 2 s. slower than Dan Gurney's pole time in the bright red 1047.

This time it was Ford's race almost all the way for after the flag was dropped, appropriately by Henry Ford II, only five cars ever held the lead - and four of them were Mark 2's. Initially Graham Hill led in XGT-2, the silver Alan Mann car, but third time round

pole man Dan Gurney was in front in the car he shared with Jerry Grant and for the first five hours either they or Miles/Hulme in 1015, the pale blue Shelby car, led the race - except for a few laps at around 1 1/2 hours when the first fuel stops temporarily handed the lead to the 330P3 Ferrari of Rodriguez/Ginther. The same Ferrari led again at 10.00 pm when the Ford's started pitting for routine brake pad changes, but by 11.00 pm Miles/Hulme were in front again and by midnight the Gurney/Grant car was lying second.

By 2.00 am the two leaders had exchanged and re-exchanged places and had

Through the Esses - two Shelby-American cars (1046 ahead) chase a Ferrari P4 in the early stages of the 1966 race. The Ferrari had a more sophisticated engine but lacked sheer cubic capacity.

been joined in third spot by McLaren/Amon in 1046. Initially running eighth, 1046 had spent the last four hours running fourth or fifth. A few laps later any threat the Fords had, apart from their own reliability, was over with the retirement from fourth place of the Rodriguez/Ginther Ferrari. This also moved Bucknum/Hutcherson in Holman and Moody's gold 1016 into fourth.

The next few hours saw no change in the top four places but by 8.00 am, two-thirds distance, McLaren/Amon had taken over the lead in 1046 from Gurney/Grant and Miles/Hulme. Bucknum/Hutcherson were still running fourth.

The only real blow Ford suffered from here on was the retirement at 9.30 am with overheating of the Gurney/Grant car which had again retaken the lead. This still left Ford in a very strong position however, and for the next 4½ hours it was the Mark 2's of McLaren/Amon, Miles/Hulme and Bucknum/Hutcherson which led Le Mans and it began to look as if this might be the line-up till the finish. However, with two hours to go and as rain began to fall, it was again Miles/Hulme who headed the leader board.

But if Ford were not to suffer any further blows, the same could not be said for two of their drivers, Miles and Hulme. For back-stage it had been decided to hold a staged finale, bunching all three cars up for a dead-heat finish for the tremendous publicity impact it would have, and as the race drew to a close the drivers were instructed accordingly. So the spectators were treated to the sight of three Mark 2's circling together for the last few laps before their final approach, lights ablaze through the rain, to take the chequered flag, with Miles easing off at the last minute to let McLaren catch him at the line.

So Ford had finally won Le Mans and pulled off a tremendous publicity stunt in the process - but they had also robbed Ken Miles, already the victor at Daytona and Sebring, of an incredible triple crown. For a dead-heat turned out to be an impossibility, as in such an event the car which had started further back in the grid - in this case McLaren/Amon's 1046 - would obviously have covered a greater distance. So Miles/ Hulme were relegated to second place with the Kiwis in 1046 declared the outright winners of the 34th Le Mans 24 hour endurance race.

A sad epitaph to this was Ken Miles's tragic death two months later while testing a J car for Ford.

The seeds of confusion which until recently shrouded the fate of Ford's first Le Mans winner were sown soon after the race in several ways. Firstly, in America two of the other 1966 Le Mans Mark 2's - GT40 P/ 1032 and XGT-3 - were turned into lookalikes of the winning car and used on the show circuit. 1032 in fact later became the

main source of confusion as it remained in its lookalike trim and gradually seemed to adopt the mantle of "Le Mans Winner" - despite the fact that its stripes were white rather than silver. Meanwhile in England Ford UK's linden green former press car GT40 P/1008 had also been turned into a 1046 clone and had joined the show circuit, although it was strictly a non-running example.

The confusion surrounding 1046's fate was then further fuelled by 1046 itself, for far from being cosseted as a Le Mans winner, it in fact became the main test hack for the following season. Its first outing (now fitted with engine number AX-316-1-49 which had clocked up four hours at Le Mans in the Foyt/Bucknum Holman and Moody prepared 1032, before its transmission blew) was only a short undocumented pre-test on October 31 in advance of the first serious test of the programme at Riverside Raceway in Arizona from November 7 - 16. This saw 1046 running alongside J-3, the latest of the J cars, Ford's alternative to the Mark 2. These cars were manufactured by a technique more associated with aircraft construction than that of racing cars, the chassis being fabricated from adhesive bonded aluminium honeycomb sandwich sections - the aluminium used being of 016 inch thickness. These cars were considerably lighter than the Mark 2's and had a lot of backing in the Ford echelons - which would prove well founded when the successor to the J car, the Mark 4, won Le Mans in 1967. But meanwhile back to Riverside.

Most of 1046's track time was taken up with comparisons of manual and automatic transmissions and testing various brake configurations, and in fact due to bad weather and track availability only six days of testing were possible. Main test drivers were Lloyd Ruby and A J Foyt with 73 and 57 laps respectively, but Bruce McLaren also turned in 25 laps and Mario Andretti a further three. This total of 158 laps was 43 more than the J car managed and the Mark 2's performance was also better. The main conclusion of the test regarding 1046 was that a lightweight body would have to be made for the Mark 2 as the car was far too heavy.

The Riverside test brought the end of Shelby-American's involvement with 1046, for immediately afterwards it was handed over to Holman and Moody for preparation for the next test in the programme, a 17 day stint at Daytona commencing December 5. And the Charlotte, North Carolina, outfit really set about their new ward, for when it rolled out into the Florida sunshine it was a much changed car - except for still being in its black and silver livery. The most obvious changes were a seven inch reduction in the length of the tail - nothing to do with aerodynamics, just a way of reducing the car's weight - and the removal of the rear deck

engine vent and brake air scoops, panels now being riveted over the holes, but a further 27 modifications had been carried out with the most significant reading as follows:-

1, The weight saved by the shortened tail had been drastically made up by the installation of a roll cage made out of 1¾ inch diameter 90 gauge steel tubing.

2, The normal fibreglass dash panel had gone, in favour of an aluminium panel in front of the driver which housed all the gauges, with a further angled panel to the left which grouped all the switches together, close to the driver's left hand.

3, The central tunnel which housed the water pipes had been removed and the pipes relocated well away from the driver down the left side of the cockpit.

4, The battery had been relocated behind the passenger's seat - along with all the electrical components, mounted on a common panel.

5, The fuel pumps were now submerged.

Drivers for 1046 were again Foyt and Ruby and although they only clocked up 14 hours running time between them, with the car suffering various problems which included alternator failure, water pump failure, fuel pick-up problems and gear selection difficulties. However the car's performance along with that of Shelby's team spare 1015 - brought in when J-3 was laid up for repairs - was sufficient to convince Ford to stick with a team of Mark 2's to get the 1967 season underway.

The weekend of February 4 - 5 saw 1046 taking part in its second - and as it would prove, last - race, the Daytona 24 hours. One of a three car Holman and Moody team, it differed little internally from its December test trim apart from having one of the new twin four-barrel Holley carburetted iron-headed engines - in its case number AX-316-2-86. The new engine weighed 80 lbs more than its aluminium-headed predecessor, but produced 530 bhp, 45 more than the unit which won Le Mans. Outwardly, however, the car had changed quite a bit. The rear deck brake air scoops and engine vent had reappeared and were mounted once again on a standard length (though much lighter, as was the whole body of the car) tail section which now incorporated a moulded-in contoured lip as on the GT40 production car, rather than the previous screw mounted flat adjustable spoiler. In addition 1046's livery had reversed as it was now finished in silver with twin black pinstripes.

The Daytona 24 hours, however, was not to be 1046's race, or for that matter the race of any of the other Mark 2's as a faulty batch of transmissions - including nine spares, all of which were used - claimed the cars one by one with only Shelby's yellow 1012 making it to the flag in seventh place courtesy of a transmission from an earlier batch snaffled from a test car Ford still had at the track. 1046, driven once again by Lloyd Ruby, this time teamed with Denis Hulme, lasted till dawn and was the fourth Mark 2 to chew up its replacement transmission.

After the Daytona debacle the J car project began to gain momentum and most of the effort was concentrated in that direction. However, the Mark 2 was still considered a worthwhile bet and 1046 was one of three Holman and Moody prepared cars (the others being 1012 and 1016) which were back at Daytona on March 21 for the start of a week long test session.

Once again much had changed in 1046's configuration since its previous outing. The whole front of the car looked different with the forward radiator air exit opened up with the removal of the bottom bar, and the brake ducts on either side covered over - the air now being picked up behind the radiator. The passenger door had been cut away to allow a luggage box to be relocated (the spare wheel later moved to the space vacated in the tail). The rear spoiler had reverted to the older screw mounted adjustable style and the rear wings had been reshaped. In this trim all three cars were basically in Mark 2B configuration, but the term was not officially designated until the following month at Sebring.

Again Ruby was the principal driver, joined on this occasion by Skip Scott and Peter Revson. Regular drivers of the successful Essex Wire entered GT40s back in 1966, this would be their first taste of the 427 powered version. And they didn't get much of a taste, as 1046 accounted for only five hours of track time over the five days

with 1012 managing even less and 1016 only clocking up 130 laps, 127 fewer than the only Mark 4 in attendance - as the new aerodynamically clothed J car was now officially known. (1012 might have clocked up more track time but for the unfortunate Peter Revson all but destroying it in a spectacular accident when the car went airborne after a tyre burst. Incredibly, and thanks to the new roll cage, Revson escaped almost unhurt).

And that Daytona test proved to be the end of 1046's active involvement in the Ford racing programme, for while 1016 went on to take part in the Le Mans trials, 1046 was never used again. Instead it sat in Holman and Moody's workshops and was gradually stripped down, initially as parts were required for cars which were still being used in the programme. Eventually, as not much more than a bare chassis and with nothing (and no-one) to suggest its former glory as a Le Mans winner, it was sold off to David Brown in Tampa, Florida. The car was then built up in almost Mark 2A trim and finished in a very pale metallic green.

It was next sold to Eo Zamerelli in Cleveland, Ohio, who then had Holman and Moody's Freddy McCall - who had done most of the original rebuild - reconstruct it as a luxury road car complete with a dash-mounted closed-circuit rear view TV monitor, the camera for which was strapped to the central bar of the roll cage (cut away down the left hand side for the purpose). The camera looked back through a neatly formed if rather incongruous looking bubble fitted to the centre rear of the roof. Colour was a vivid metalflake gold.

This then was the rather ignominious fate of Ford's first Le Mans winner. But not for long, as the car then moved to Steve Juda in New York - and then back once again to Freddy McCall whom Juda commissioned to put it back in standard Mark 2 trim. However, half-way through the work the car was sold yet again and the new owner called a halt to the rebuild. Eventually, in 1980, it was acquired by Bob Richmond in New York (in a deal which included 1074 and J-4) and was crated up and shipped out to Belgium for storage as an investment, until its sale on November 8 1983 (again along with 1074 and J-4) to George Stauffer, a Wisconsin based businessman and fast rising star of the American classic car dealer network.

Stauffer recruited the help of the author to find if what he was buying was indeed the Le Mans winner, and although it was no simple task, through the meticulous records which were kept of all the Shelby-American and Holman and Moody testing modifications to the car, and after exhaustive photographic research the proof finally came together.

George still owns 1046 but has as yet done little to it. But the search for the necessary parts goes on relentlessly and some day, hopefully not too far in the future, GT40 P/1046 will once again appear in the trim in which it won Le Mans for the Ford Motor Company on June 19 1966.

Heading for the historic win - P/1046 the McLaren/Amon Ford Mark 2 (car number 2), splashes towards success. Ford tried to stage a dead-heat but the ACO wouldn't play ball...

FORD MKIV

Developed from the experimental J car seen at the Le Mans test weekend in 1966, the Ford MkIV had a chassis built from bonded and riveted aluminium honeycomb sheets, a material in common use in the aircraft industry but radical in its use in automotive construction. As in the earlier GT40, and its derivatives, side boxes formed the fuel cells, transverse bulkheads between these sponsons tying together the tub, which carried a sturdy roll cage around the cockpit area. The engine transmission and rear suspension were fixed in place (as on the GT40) by a fabricated steel frame. The use of aluminium honeycomb provided a massive 300 lb weight saving over the MkII. The engine was that used in the MkII, a 7.0 litre V8, although the use of a pair of four choke Holley carburettors had boosted power to 500 bhp at 5000r.p.m. A Ford-designed automatic two speed gearbox from the J car was eventually discarded in favour of the tried and tested T44 4 speed 'box and Long dry twin-plate clutch.

Suspension was taken wholesale from the MkII. The body work was more streamlined with a narrow cockpit surround improving air penetration. The water radiator remained front mounted with a single top exit ahead of the windscreen. The large rear bodywork scoops of the MkII were replaced with less-drag-creating ducts in the doors and sides of the cockpit roof. An adjustable spoiler was fitted across the rear as on previous cars.

At the test weekend the two MkIVs present were beaten on times by a pair of Ferraris but significantly the Fords were the only cars to be clocked at over 200 mph on the Mulsanne straight. Returning to Western France for the race four MkIVs spearheaded the Ford entry for 1967. Two cars were run by Shelby and two by Holman and Moody. Dominant in practice, the race became the expected Ford against Ferrari showdown with Ford holding the upper hand. The brute power of the big, low revving, pushrod V8 mated to a lightweight chassis was too much for the Maranello challenge to withstand. By the end of the

race the Shelby car of Gurney and Le Mans debutant Foyt had a five lap lead over the second placed Ferrari. The second Shelby car of McLaren/Donohue finished fourth, its bodywork secured by copious amounts of tape and (as legend has it) mechanics trouser belts!

The Holman and Moody cars were considerably less fortunate: Hulme set a succession of new lap records in the first few hours of the race, only for his car to be retired when co-driver Ruby damaged the sump in an off road excursion. In the other car Andretti spun at 4am in the Esses and hit the safety bank triggering a multiple accident which eliminated two other Fords in addition to his own.

And with the Big Banger ban, this ended the Ford MkIV story.

FORD	
Mk4 - 1967	90 degree V8
Alloy honeycomb monocoque	7.0 litres
Suspension:	Iron block
wishbone front	Carburettor
wishbone rear	16 valves
Engine unstressed	Pushrod
Ford gearbox	Unblown
Flat bottom	500 b.h.p.

HOWMET TX

In late 1967, utilising a conventional multi-tubular spaceframe chassis supplied by McKee Engineering, Ray Heppenstall built an aluminium bodied coupe for the Howmet Corporation. Designated the TX, the car was powered by a Continental TS325-1 gas turbine engine, more commonly utilised to drive helicopter main rotors. Under the new rules that were to apply in 1968 the engine would have an equivalency rating of 3.0 litres. Weighing a mere 170 lbs, it produced 330 bhp at around 6800 rpm (after reduction gearing). An inherent throttle lag problem was addressed by the use of a waste gate which varied gas flow to the turbine.

Suspension was conventional by wishbone and coil spring dampers at the front, single upper links, lower wishbones and spring/dampers at the rear. The aluminium body was fitted with a roof mounted air collector reminiscent of the Chaparral 2D and was almost completely lacking a rear panel to allow dissipation of turbine heat .

Encouraging early tests at Daytona at the end of 1967 saw the go ahead given for a full season of competition in 1968. Early races showed up shortcomings in handling and throttle control resulting in a number of accidents. Nevertheless, two cars were entered for Le Mans with Heppenstall himself sharing with Thompson, the second car driven by Tullius and Dibley (the latter appropriately an airline pilot). Qualifying in midfield, both cars hit trouble early on in the race. Dibley's broke a rear hub which was rebuilt, albeit time consumingly in the pits while the Heppenstall car was plagued by a fuel control valve fault that restricted the car to sub 100 mph runs along the Mulsanne straight. The Dibley car resumed after three hours work only to be excluded due to insufficient distance covered at the am. check. To complete the tale of misery Thompson rolled the other car at Indianapolis corner and thus retired.

Despite a couple of minor race wins in America during the season, overall problems outweighed any advantages and the fascinating project was abandoned.

HOWMET	CONTINENTAL
TX - 1968	gas turbine engine
Steel spaceframe	= 3.0 litres
Suspension:	330 b.h.p.
wishbone front	
wishbone rear	
Engine unstressed	
Continental gearbox	
Flat bottom	

MATRA MS630

Formed from the remnants of Rene Bonnet Prototypes in 1964 (a company with a Le Mans tradition but little in the way of success), Matra Sports produced a trio of 2.0 litre, V8 B.R.M. engined coupes for the 1966 Le Mans race, all three retiring before half-distance. 1967 saw the introduction of a 4.7 litre Ford V8 engined chassis. However the B.R.M. engined cars were entered at Le Mans, again unsuccessfully.

For 1968 the Ford chassis, type MS630, was fitted with Matra's new Formula One engine. Financed by the French government, the 60 degree V12 MS9 motor displaced 2,999cc and featured four valves per cylinder, twin overhead camshafts on each bank of cylinders and Lucas fuel injection. Transmission was by the familiar five speed ZF unit. For endurance events the quoted power output was 380bhp at 9,000rpm. The chassis, a multi-tubular space frame, employed conventional wishbone suspension with combined coil spring and damper units all round. Water and oil radiators were side mounted ahead of the rear wheels to allow the use of a sleek nose, improving aerodynamics. In the practice sessions the car achieved fifth fastest time driven by Grand Prix debutants Servoz-Gavin and Pescarolo. In the race the car was running in second place before a series of punctures caused by accident debris

gave rise to a small electrical fire that ended a fine effort at 11am on Sunday.

1969 produced a futuristic coupe with bodywork based on the aerodynamic theories of Robert Choulet, a former associate of Charles Deutsch (builder of the super-streamlined CD Le Mans cars. The MS640 used much the same running gear as its predecessor covered with bulbous bodywork that featured tall vertical tail fins to aid straight line stability. Alas, the car was written off and Pescarolo was injured in an accident on the Mulsanne straight during testing. After investigation, the 640 project was set aside, the 1969 entry comprising three spyder cars plus a slightly modified 630 for Guichet and Vaccarella (car 32) winners for Ferrari in 1964. A consistent run netted sixth place at the finish for the coupe.

MATRA	
630 - 1968	60 degree V12
Steel spaceframe	3.0 litres
Suspension:	Alloy block
wishbone front	Fuel injected
wishbone rear	48 valves
Engine semi-stressed	d.o.h.c.
ZF gearbox	Unblown
Flat bottom	380 b.h.p.

PORSCHE 908

Introduced at the 1968 Le Mans test weekend, the Porsche 908 was the German company's first full blooded 3.0 litre prototype design. The eight cylinder engine had a magnesium alloy crankcase with alloy cylinders and twin cam heads in the familiar horizontally opposed configuration. Displacing 2926cc with a bore and stroke of 84 x 66mm, the power output was quoted as 335bhp at 8500 rpm for the two valve per cylinder motor. Bosch fuel injection developed on a preceeding six cylinder engine was incorporated and transmission was by a four plate Borg and Beck clutch and Porsche's own six speed gearbox.

The chassis was a tubular spaceframe, similar to the earlier 2.2 litre 907, gas pressurised to enable cracks to be detected via pressure loss. The front suspension was a conventional twin wishbone arrangement, while at the rear were single upper links, lower wishbones and radius arms with the spring/dampers. The car ran on 15 inch cast magnesium wheels and was braked by outboard mounted ventilated ATE discs. The glassfibre bodywork, again bearing a resemblance to the 907, featured gull wing doors, front mounted oil radiator and, for Le Mans, a sleek long tail section.

All four cars entered were in long tail mode with twin vertical fins on which was mounted a wide fixed aerofoil with suspension activated mobile flaps, a system originiated on an earlier hill climb car to equalise rear wheel loadings.

In the race engine vibrations, a recurrent problem in the 908's first season of racing, caused alternator problems which decimated the quartet and caused the retirement of three cars. The survivor, driven by Stommelen/Neerpasch, came home third, albeit behind one of the three 2.0 litre 907 back up cars entered by private teams (with works assistance).

Returning in 1969, the 908 had benefitted from a full season of racing development in both spyder and coupe form. Three coupes were entered as part of a six car works entry which also included two 917s and a 908 spyder. In the race a 917 led for 21 hours. Then its retirement left the coupe of Herrmann/Larrousse and a Gulf Ford GT40 to fight it out to the flag, a battle that Porsche was to lose by less than 2 seconds after 24 hours of racing. The coupe of Schutz/Mitter had been destroyed in a lurid accident at the Mulsanne kink which broke the car to pieces and sent Schutz tumbling down the road, incredibly without injury. Lins/Kauhsen in the remaining coupe had retired with clutch failure when running second to the 917.

The 908 continued to appear in spyder form in the following seasons while a 908 long tail coupe made a sentimental journey back to the Sarthe circuit in 1972 when a car prepared and run by "holidaying" works mechanics on behalf of the Jo Siffert team finished third behind the Matras in the hands of Joest/Weber/Casoni.

PORSCHE	
908 - 1968	Boxer 8
Alloy spaceframe	3.0 litres
Suspension:	Alloy blocks
wishbone front	Fuel injected
wishbone rear	16 valves
Engine unstressed	d.o.h.c.
Porsche gearbox	Unblown
Flat bottom	335 b.h.p.

PORSCHE 917

Bursting through a loophole in the World Manufacturers Championship that permitted engines of up to 5.0 litres in cars of which twenty five or more had been built, Porsche shocked the motor racing world by announcing its type 917 at the 1969 Geneva motor show.

Externally similar to the 908, the new car was fitted with the largest air-cooled racing engine ever produced. With a magnesium crankcase and aluminium cylinder heads the flat 12 engine in its original form used many components from the 3.0 litre 908 engine, pistons and connecting rods among other internal parts which dictated a bore and stroke of 85 x 66 mm and the resultant capacity of 4494cc. Interestingly the crankshaft was formed from two separate forgings joined at a mid-point power take-off. From this a series of geared wheels fed power to twin camshafts on each head, the oil pumps, engine cooling fan, and, in addition, to a shaft below the crank which rotated a triple plate clutch and a strengthened version of the 908 gearbox. The dry sump lubricated, two valve per cylinder unit was fitted with Bosch fuel injection and dual distributor ignition.

The chassis was a tubular spaceframe with the driving position so far forward to accommodate the long engine that when seated in the car the driver's feet protruded ahead of the front wheel axis. Part of the chassis frame doubled as the plumbing system for a front mounted oil radiator, oil playing an important engine cooling role. Suspension was similar to that of the 908

and the earlier car's fifteen inch cast magnesium wheels were retained. The bodywork had a wide and low nose with the front of the windscreen between the wheel arches while a vented perspex rear window was set above the engine, in a tail that could be fitted with a bolt-on extension for faster circuits. The lower tail flanks featured a cut out ahead of the rear wheels through which the exhaust pipe for the front three cylinders on each bank was directed, the rearmost cylinders' exhaust being directed out under the tail. Aerodynamically the 917 was again similar to the 908 in its use of suspension-linked rear flaps mounted on vertical fins balanced by twin spoilers on the outer edges of the nose.

Early performances ranged from disappointing to alarming, the car inherently unstable. For the 1969 Le Mans race four 917s were entered, two long tail works cars for Elford/Attwood and Stommelen/Ahrens with a spare training car, plus the first customer car to be driven its new owner Woolfe partnered by Porsche test driver Linge. The two works cars were easily quickest in practice with the private car tenth. In the race Woolfe crashed fatally on the opening lap, while the two works cars ran impressively at the head of the field. The German crewed car set a fast early pace until it fell victim to a series of oil leaks which, despite a major rebuild of the clutch, caused its retirement during the night. The British driven car lasted right through until the twenty first hour when the clutch and gearbox malfunctioned and the car was retired having led for more than sixteen hours.

PORSCHE	
917 - 1969	180 degree V12
Alloy spaceframe	4.5 litres
Suspension:	Alloy blocks
wishbone front	fuel injected
wishbone rear	24 valves
Engine unstressed	d.o.h.c.
Porsche gearbox	Unblown
Flat bottom	550 b.h.p.

TRIFFIDS AT LE MANS

In less than two years Porsche race cars grew like Triffids, from well established small capacity class contenders into giants of the endurance circuits. With the help of contemporary engineers Piech, Mezger, Falk and Flegl, Ian Bamsey has throughly researched the story of the first Porsche giant the 917, and recounts its birth

Elephant country. Only hefty, slow turning American V8 engines had ever been seen here. The heights beyond 500bhp was territory unexplored by thoroughbred European race engines. Even the ultimate 4.0 litre, three valve Ferrari V12 had summoned no more than 450bhp countering the 530bhp of the elephantine 7.0 litre pushrod invaders from across the Atlantic. Yet here was a new German two valve V12 pushing an easy 550bhp from 4.5 litres, and it was air cooled to boot. Just like the humble Volkswagen Beetle.

Prior to the recent ban on elephants (from '68 5.0 litres was the largest capacity sports-prototype class) the emphasis on sheer size saw Ford win Le Mans with an engine producing a mere 76bhp per litre. The rival Ferrari V12 offered a more respectable 112bhp per litre and the shortage of Italian 'cubes' was also partly offset by a lighter car. Nevertheless, the '67 P4 weighed over 950kg. The '68 regulations governing 50-off cars accepted 5.0 litres with a minimum weight of 800kg.

No existing or foreseeable 50-off car offered more than 76bhp per litre. We are considering 4.5/5.0 litre Ford and Chevrolet V8 engines producing less than 400bhp (plus an old 3.3 litre Ferrari V12). Nevertheless, a hypothetical 50-off 5.0 litre car with an engine as efficient as that of the P4 would boast 560bhp and could, in theory, run at 800kg. And the P4's engine wasn't particularly efficient by the standards of '68: the new Cosworth V8 produced 450bhp from only 3.0 litres - 150bhp. per litre...

Engine technology was moving fast in the mid/late Sixties. More valves and more efficient combustion chamber shapes, together with twin overhead camshafts for each cylinder bank, fuel injection and transistorised ignition systems were behind soaring power per litre figures. The mould for the classic four valve race engine was set in this period and the trendsetting Cosworth DFV would live on for years to come.

One off prototypes were limited to 3.0

Sixteen cylinders, 4.5 litres and only an overhead plastic fan to keep it all cool (though a fair proportion of heat was extracted via the oil system).

litres for '68: the rule makers were ensuring Le Mans cars would be hard pressed to reach 450bhp and survive 24 hours. At least until such time as someone set out to homologate a car with a more advanced engine. Surely a two valve air cooled engine couldn't fit the bill? Porsche produced air cooled race engines to promote its air cooled road sports cars. Air cooling didn't offer significant advantages but neither did it offer significant disadvantages by pre-Cosworth standards and, with clever materials technology, it did allow a lightweight unit to be produced.

Porsche had a racing version of its production 2.0 litre, two valve, six cylinder 'boxer' engine with a cast magnesium crankcase and Beetle-style 'upright' cooling fan. With two plugs per cylinder fired by Bosch transistor ignition and twin Weber carburettors it produced 210bhp (105bhp per litre). In '68 the marque had followed that with a 3.0 litre, eight cylinder boxer featuring twin overhead cams, transistorised ignition and fuel injection. Still with upright fan and essentially simple elements it produced 335bhp : 112bhp per litre.

Although its eight cylinder engine matched the standard of the beached P4, Porsche knew it could do better. More than two valves per cylinder were out of the question due to the need for cooling air to circulate around the head but a horizontal (overhead) fan could provide better cooling and a 180 degree V12 rather than the traditional boxer configuration would provide better internal ventilation, releasing significantly more power.

The problem was one of cost: the compromises of the 1967-designed eight cylinder boxer were in response to financial considerations. A backer was needed, and if the car was to be homologated (hence 5.0 litres) it had better be a big backer. Early in '68 the homologation quantity was cut to 25 units but that still represented a massive investment for a brand new sports-prototype. Could such an investment be justified?

Porsche Technical Director Ferdinand Piech had been getting an ever increasing allowance for his racing operation but this was beyond Porsche's resources. However, the grandson of Beetle creator Professor Ferdinand Porsche (son of Louise who co-founded the Porsche marque with brother Ferry), Ferdinand Piech had powerful connections at Volkswagen. The mass manufacturer bought the idea of a new prototype to win Le Mans with an air cooled engine...

The expensive go-ahead was given in July '68, soon after the homologation quantity reduction. Piech wanted above all else to win Le Mans and this awesome 5.0 litre 'Group 4' project had that as its specific goal, as surely as had the 7.0 litre Fords. On slower sinuous circuits a flyweight, agile

450bhp 3.0 litre prototype might be as competitive as an 800kg. 5.0 litre rival but at Le Mans there was no substitute for sheer horsepower.

The danger was that, while the Porsche 917 should, on paper, easily set standards for Le Mans performance to which no 3.0 litre challenger could aspire, it was surely only a matter of time before Ferrari produced its own 25-off prototype with four valve V12. If Cosworth had found 150bhp per litre from a four valve engine there was no way that Ferrari was going to fail to improve significantly upon the 112bhp per litre of the P4 engine. As Porsche couldn't produce a four valver and retain air cooling it had to accept that the 5.0 litre Ferrari, when it arrived, would almost certainly

Vic Elford led the 1969 Le Mans 24 hour race overnight in the 917, gentle driving coaxing the too new car further than its engineers thought possible, if not far enough to win.

boast a better output.

The 917 was designed to be light for maximum performance and for improved durability and fuel consumption and to have low drag, again for improved fuel consumption (saving pit stops), and for higher Mulsanne speed. Low weight and low drag had long been central to the Porsche racing car design creed. The marque had traditionally fielded small capacity endurance cars and extensive research in these areas had helped compensate for lack of muscle.

The 917 boasted a light (magnesium crankcase/aluminium cylinders) air cooled engine, and a light chassis that similarly employed Porsche's advanced materials know how. The result: a total dry weight very little over the target 800kg. figure. Like the engine, the chassis made extensive use of exotic metals (including titanium springs, hubs and anti roll bars) and it employed an aluminium spaceframe with g.r.p. body panels bonded to it. To save weight the traditional Porsche prototype wheelbase of 2300mm. was retained, in spite of the longer block. That set the driver well forward in the chassis.

In essence, the chassis was a straightforward development of that of the 908, with emphasis again on low drag. Devoid of spoilers, with a bolt-on Le Mans long tail extension the car had a quoted drag co-efficient of 0.33, 0.8% lower than that of the 908. It was estimated that it would reach 236m.p.h. on the Mulsanne. To provide high speed stability (and downforce was not a serious part of the equation) Porsche added aircraft-style trim tabs to the end of its long tail, these taking the form of flaps that moved in sympathy with the suspension. The idea was to aerodynamically-counter pitch changes, and the front suspension featured 50% anti-dive to the same end.

The distinctive flaps had been seen on the 908. The radical departure of the 917 was the abandoning of the traditional boxer configuration. With the boxer configuration - opposite pistons moving inwards towards each other rather than sharing a crankpin and thus moving in the same direction - internal ventilation was a major problem. By creating a 180 degree V12 Porsche reduced inner compression: air pressure and turbulence in the crankcase were reduced, facilitating the creation of a good oil mist and minimising power losses. Further, with six rather than 12 crankpins the bearing requirement was reduced and it was possible to provide more robust webs and to increase the width of both big end and main bearings (while still enjoying reduced frictional loss) to improve lubrication and reduce oil throughput.

Good balance was ensured by a crank configuration identical to that for an in line six, with each pin at 120 degrees from its neighbour and pairing rods reduced the overall shaft length. However, due to the need for cooling air to circulate around each cylinder the bores had to be widely spaced and with six cylinders on each side shaft length was such that calculations suggested torsional vibration could be a serious problem. The only way to avoid the problem was to take the power off the centre of the shaft.

The amplitude of torsional vibration of the shaft reduced towards the centre where there was a point of interference. Engine designer Hans Mezger positioned a power take-off pinion at this point, ensuring the

drive would be vibration-free throughout the rev range. This was a major advantage for the camshaft drive, allowing a gear system to be employed without fear of a vibration problem.

A significant advantage of the central drive pinion was that it left both ends of the shaft free to accept an axial big end lubrication feed. In other Porsche engines the oil had to be fed in radially and consequently had to have sufficient pressure to counteract the centrifugal force of the shaft. The 917 ran a significantly lower oil pressure and was designed to be as dry as possible to minimise splashing losses. Six scavenge pumps were employed.

A horizontal cooling fan and an efficient oil system were both important cooling measures. Porsche air cooled engines were part oil cooled but whereas earlier, vertical fan, compromise engines had been 30-35% oil cooled the 917 was only 15-20% oil cooled, Mezger reckons. Driven by gears, the horizontal fan absorbed 17bhp which compares favourably with the amount of power that would otherwise have been wasted pushing a large water radiator through the air. And the weight of water jackets and a water system was saved. As usual, the new Porsche engine was light, with a magnesium crankcase and an extensive use of exotic metals, including titanium, throughout.

As far as possible, the 917 engine was derived from proven technology: the reciprocating gear, the cylinders (aluminium with chrome plated bores) and the two valve heads were adapted from the 908. Even 908 bore and stroke dimensions were retained, 85 x 66mm. producing a 4.5 litre capacity - 5.0 litres could wait! As we have noted, the 908 produced 120bhp. per litre - with the new 180 degree V12 Porsche was looking for something better and one improvement was a slightly narrower valve angle for a more compact (but still 'orange peel' shape, with domed piston crown) combustion chamber.

Bench testing commenced in December 1968 and it took little coaxing for the output to match the power per litre of the 908 with 542bhp The engine ran a 10.5:1 compression ratio and produced maximum power at 8,400rpm. Mezger reported that "from the start it was better in its mechanical behaviour than any previous Porsche engine. The central drive was the answer". With the vibration free power take-off, rigid gear drive and inflexible valve actuation due to the use of bucket tappets, he reckoned the valve gear was "an optimum solution".

By Le Mans 1969 power was well in excess of 550bhp: pure elephant grunt from a car significantly lighter than the outlawed American machines. And, with development, there was more to come. 600bhp was well within grasp...

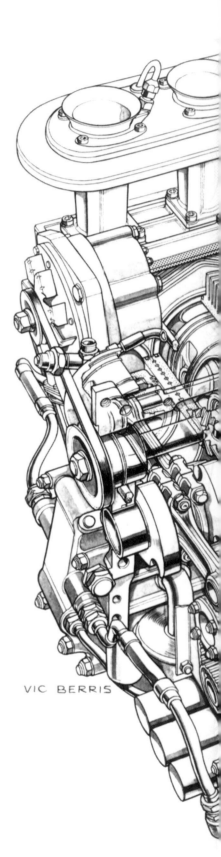

VIC BERRIS

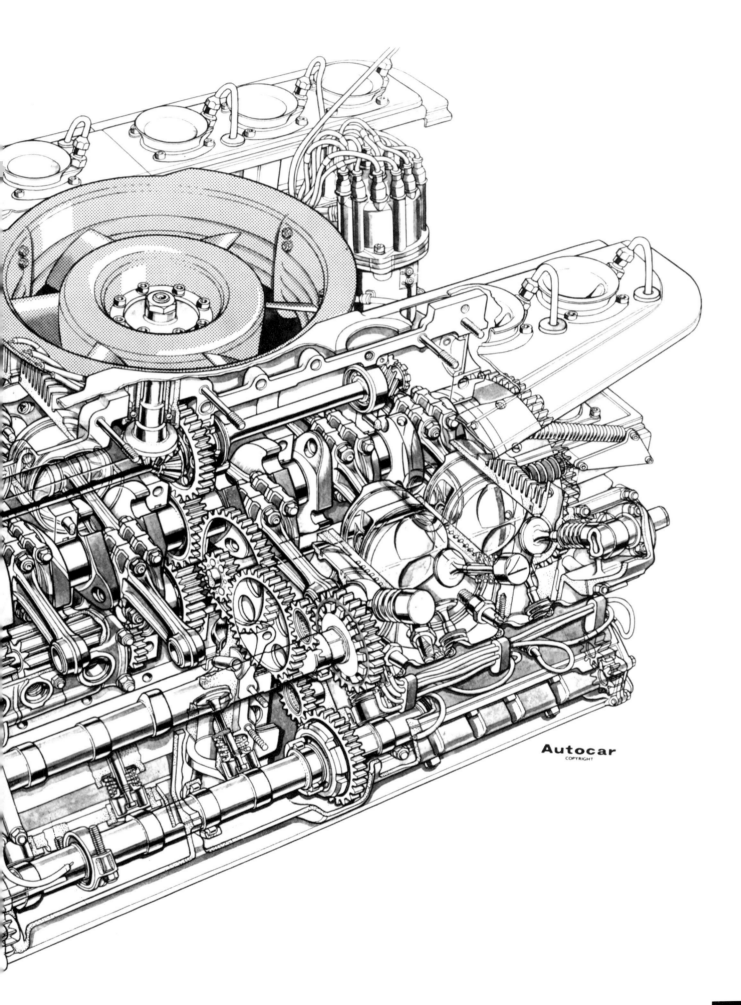

PORSCHE 917K

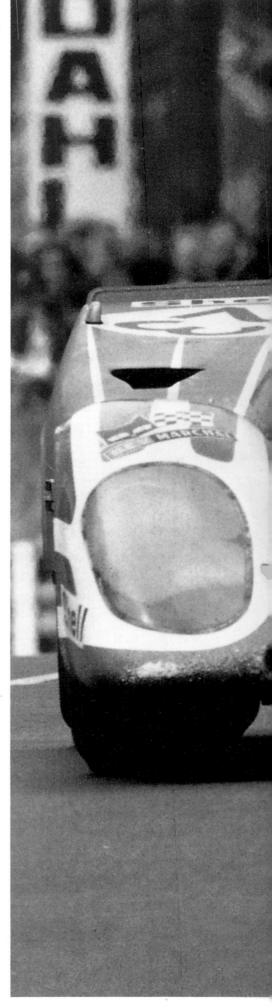

Following the last round of the 1969 Manufacturers Championship, the Porsche 917 was subjected to a development programme with the aim of turning it from a powerful but unweildy monster into a world beater. At the Oesterreichring in October of that year a new nose and tail section were devised in conjunction with members of the J.W. Automotive team, who were to run the works team in 1970. The modifications transformed the previously evil handling with a coincidental weight saving. The gearbox was altered to a four speed configuration, the tremendous torque of the flat 12 engine allowing first gear to be omitted on most circuits. Later, a hub redesign, resulting from failures early in the 1970 season, made possible the use of Girling disc brakes in place of the original ATE equipment (as retained by the private Porsche Salzburg team). A separate oil plumbing system reduced cockpit overheating, a problem caused by routing oil from the front mounted radiator through the chassis tubes on the original car.

In the first races of 1970 the 917 continued to use the original 4.5 litre engine which was rated at 550bhp at 8750rpm, before a 4907cc unit became available with a power increase of 40bhp. At Le Mans JWA entered three cars as per its contract with Porsche, while three cars were also entered by Porsche Salzburg, a single car by Martini International and the Finnish AAW team. The Wyer cars were all in short tail Kurz form as were two of the Salzburg cars and the AAW chassis, the others running long tail bodywork as tried at the test weekend in April.

One Salzburg 'K' was damaged in a accident during practice and withdrawn. The race was run mainly in attrociously wet conditions favouring the higher downforce short tail cars. The JW car of Siffert/Redman with a 4.9 litre engine led from the second hour until the Swiss missed a gear and damaged the engine. The Rodriguez/Kinnunen car had retired after just over an hour when the distributor drive broke, and completing a miserable race for the team its

4.5 litre car shared by Hobbs/Hailwood was crashed by the latter in a heavy rainstorm during the fourth hour.

The Finnish car was abandoned when a tyre burst on the Mulsanne straight and wrecked the rear suspension and body in the ninth hour. Splashing through the water and carnage the Salzburg 917K of Hermann and Attwood inherited the lead from Siffert and held it through to the end of the race to score Porsche's first Le Mans victory.

In 1971 the 917K provided back up for long tail cars at Le Mans. Development work on the Kurz in the aerodynamic field brought about the introduction of a lower rear deck with vertical tail fins which increased revs without loss of straightline stability. Engine changes increased the displacement to 4999cc with new Nikasil cylinders power rising to 620bhp. Prudence, however, dictated the use of a slightly smaller 4907cc Nikasil engine for Le Mans. A single Kurz apiece was entered by JWA and Martini International with a slow Swiss-entered car completing the 917K ranks. The long tail 917s fell by the wayside the Martini Kurz driven by Marko/Van Lennep finishing first ahead of the Gulf Kurz of Attwood/Muller. The Swiss car retired, in part due to a shortage of spares after gearbox problems with five hours left to run. Regulation changes coming into effect at the start of 1972 outlawed the 917: an era had ended.

PORSCHE	
917K - 1970	180 degree V12
Alloy spaceframe	4.9 litres
Suspension:	Alloy blocks
wishbone front	Fuel injected
wishbone rear	24 valves
Engine unstressed	d.o.h.c.
Porsche gearbox	Unblown
Flat bottom	590 b.h.p.

PORSCHE 917LH

By the 1970 Le Mans race extensive further development of the original long tail Porsche 917 had been carried out by the factory in conjunction with the S.E.R.A. design company run by Charles Deutsch, designer of the series of streamlined D.B. and C.D. cars from the late Forties to the mid-Sixties. Accidents during private testing and the Le Mans test weekend influenced a decision by the J.W. Automotive team to run short tail 917Ks. Two Langhecks were therefore allocated to the Porsche Salzburg and the Martini International team.

The cars they were to use had the same chassis dimensions, cockpit structure and mid-section as the 917K with lengthened front and rear bodywork. The nose panel had a concave, downforce producing upper surface perforated by twin radiator vents expelling hot air either side of the windscreen. The tail section rose over the rear wheel arches on which were located air scoops for brake and transmission cooling. Aft of the wheels, the rear deck took on a concave shape surmounted by twin vertical fins which carried a full width adjustable aerofoil.

The Porsche computer predicted a top speed of 239 mph on the Mulsanne straight: 235 mph was achieved in reality. Running with a 4.9 litre engine, the Salzburg car of Elford/Ahrens beat off a strong Ferrari challenge for pole position and led for the first two hours of the race before being passed by one of the JWA 917Ks. Later slow punctures and problems with a headlamp mounting dropped the car back to fifth place at midnight. By the early morning it was back up to second place when Ahrens collided with a slower car and lost time having damaged bodywork repaired. Just after 8.30am it was retired with a broken valve spring.

The Martini car, fitted with the older 4.5 litre engine, encountered misfire and electrical problems caused by the almost incessant rain but managed to finish in second place driven by Larrousse/Kauhsen.

When the Langhecks were wheeled out for the 1971 test weekend a great deal more refinement had obviously taken place. A new nose section with a squarer lower portion gave improved downforce at the front end while a revised tail with partially faired-in rear wheels and revised rear cooling ducts improved the air flow over the rear wing. The new specification 917LH was blindingly fast. Oliver reaching 240 mph during practice, and lapped the circuit six seconds faster than Elford's 1970 pole time.

Three Langhecks were entered for the race, and Rodriguez, in one of the Wyer cars took pole poistion with Elford alongside and Siffert in the second Gulf car third. This trio led the field away from the start before Siffert and Elford were both delayed by minor electrical problems the Elford's engine broke. The wheel spats caused the rear hubs to overheat and thirty laps were lost by Siffert as the fault was diagnosed and a rebuild carried out. Rodriguez/Oliver contineud to lead through the nine hour mark until struck by a similar suspension problem. Now used to the task the team completed reparis in just 22 minutes and the car dropped only three places to fourth. In the thirteenth hour Rodriguez suffered a fractured oil line on the Mulsanne and before the Mexican could nurse the car back to its pit all engine lubricant had been pumped out with terminal effect.

By the early hours of Sunday Siffert/Bell Langheck was back into sixth place but a cracked crankcase and loss of oil put the car out with six hours remaining.

PORSCHE	
917LH - 1970	180 degree V12
Alloy spaceframe	4.9 litres
Suspension:	Alloy blocks
wishbone front	Fuel injected
wishbone rear	24 valves
Engine unstressed	d.o.h.c.
Porsche gearbox	Unblown
Flat bottom	580 b.h.p.

PORSCHE 917-20

Der Trüffel-Jäger von Zuffenhausen

Introduced at the 1971 Test Weekend, the Porsche 917-20 was a factory design exercise to produce a car with the stability of the short tail 917K and the low drag coefficient of the 917 Langheck.

A relaxation of homologation rules in the final season of Group Five allowed Porsche to build a one off car to test its aerodynamic theories. The design work was carried out in conjunction with S.E.R.A. which had also contributed to the Langheck project. The resulting car had a very wide body and an extremely short nose and tail. The lower nose area was similar to the 1971 long tail car but higher up featured heavily louvered bulbous wheel arches designed to reduce interference between the air whipped up by wheel rotation and the flow down the flanks. The cockpit area was as on a regular 917; the tail was wide with a short smooth rear deck sporting vertical fins between which was a small rear spoiler on the trailing edge of the car. The engine and running gear was standard 917.

By the time of its return to Le Mans to race the 917-20 had been painted a porcine shade of pink and was signwritten with dotted lines indicating cuts of pork as per a butcher's shop diagram. Identified on its nose as "The Truffle Pig of Zuffenhausen", its two swineherds for the weekend were to be Joest and Kauhsen, the car being entered by Martini International. Qualified seventh behind its long tail cousins the car ran strongly and was fifth at the quarter distance mark. The fan bolts that had sheared with disastrous effect on the other Martini car were looking suspect and were replaced, the car moved up to fourth after nine hours. A thirteen minute pit stop to repair a broken throttle linkage dropped the car back and shortly after returning to the race Joest crashed at Arnage when the brakes failed. Damage was negligible but the lighting had been wiped out so the car could not continue.

PORSCHE	
917/20 - 1971	180 degree V12
Alloy spaceframe	4.9 litres
Suspension:	Alloy blocks
wishbone front	Fuel injected
wishbone rear	24 valves
Engine unstressed	d.o.h.c.
Porsche gearbox	Unblown
Flat bottom	600 b.h.p.

ALPINE A220 RENAULT

Basing a car on a five year old chassis design and fitting it with an underpowered engine is not a recipe for success at Le Mans. This was the approach chosen by Societie des Automobiles Alpine in late 1967; the results speak for themselves.

With new rules restricting the prototype class to engines with a maximum capacity of three litres, Amedee Gordini produced a Renault-derived 90 V8 engine of 2986cc. Basically a pair of 1500cc engines sharing a common crankcase, the engine had a cast iron block and aluminium cylinder heads with four valves per cylinder. Disappointingly, the unit produced only 300 bhp in race trim, considerably less than its contemporaries.

The chassis was a spaceframe construction to a 1962 design by freelancer Len Terry. Like the then-current Maserati Birdcage, it featured dozens of fully triangulated small diameter tubes. Conventional wishbone suspension was fitted at each corner. A streamlined glassfibre body helped compensate for the shortfall of 100 bhp but the A211 was outclassed by all of its Group 6 rivals. Debuted at the 1967 Paris 1000 kilometre race at Montlhery the team was flattered by a seventh place finish.

A refined version, designated the A220 appeared at Monza in early 1968 with revised suspension and brakes but most noticeably with side mounted water radiators. The car retired with handling problems resulting from an accident in practice. Another qualifying accident totally destroyed the car on its next appearance at Nurburgring and it was only the rescheduling of Le Mans for September 1968 that gave the team enough time to prepare for the race.

Four 3.0 litre cars were entered and Bianchi/Depailler managed to qualify in the top ten and rose as high as fifth before crashing violently out on the Sunday morning when Bianchi suffered total brake failure. A similar fault saw to another of the quartet, while a third car retired when its headlamps failed

in the dark on the Mulsanne straight! Some honour was salvaged by the remaining car, finishing eighth.

Bodywork changes for 1969 included the mounting of the radiators at the rear, repositioning of the oil cooler in the nose and experiments with a tall rear-mounted aerofoil which was eventually discarded. Under the body the fitting of rubber bag fuel tanks and a change to Girling disc brakes reflected the extent of closed season development.

Four cars were again entered for Le Mans, three with tail mounted radiators, one to 1968 side radiator specification. A spate of mechanical failures continued the Alpine tale of woe at the Sarthe, two head gasket failures, an oil pipe breakage and bearing failure ending the challenge early on Sunday morning. After such a public disaster, the decision was taken to withdraw from racing and concentrate on rallying. Alpine would, however, return to Le Mans, and the much sought after win would finally come in 1978.

ALPINE	RENAULT
A220 - 1968	90 degree V8
Steel spaceframe	3.0 litres
Suspension:	Iron block
wishbone front	Fuel injected
wishbone rear	16 valves
Engine unstressed	d.o.h.c
ZF gearbox	Unblown
Flat bottom	300 b.h.p.

CHEVRON REPCO

A Chevron was entered for Le Mans for the first time in 1968. Based closely on the customer B8 coupe, the Le Mans runner was fitted with a Formula One-type Repco V8 rather than the usual 2.0 litre engine and was thus designated the B12. Designed by Chevron founder Derek Bennett, the attractive chassis was a multi tube spaceframe with metal plating for reinforcement and bonded in stressed floor and fuel tank. Suspension was traditional with wishbones and coil spring/damper units front and rear.

The pleasing body shape was a glassfibre moulding and allowed for a front mounted radiator while the tail section had been enlongated to accomodate the 3.0 litre V8, the chassis having been stretched by 2.5 inches. The 1966 and '67 World Championship winning engine was a 90 degree V8 with twin overhead cams which running Lucas fuel injection produced 330b.h.p. at 8,800r.p.m.

Although it had achieved such single seater success, this engine proved unreliable as an endurance power plant. In the 1968 Le Mans race the car, driven by owner John Woolfe and Martland, retired after just three hours with a blown head gasket.

CHEVRON	REPCO
B12 - 1968	90 degree V8
Steel plated spaceframe	3.0 litres
Suspension:	Alloy block
wishbone front	Fuel injected
wishbone rear	16 valves
Engine semi-stressed	d.o.h.c.
Hewland gearbox	Unblown
Flat bottom	330 b.h.p.

THE SPYDER YEARS
1972 - 1979

while another recorded the first finish for the factory with eighth place.

Porsche had run a modified 911 in the prototype class in '73 and '74 but in '75 the limited production road/race Ligier was the only enclosed car running in the top category. Matra having withdrawn from racing at the end of '74 (with a hat trick of Le Mans wins to its credit), Ligier had acquired its Gitanes sponsorship and its Technical Director Gerard Ducarouge. Two JS2s now ran with Cosworth DFV engines, backed up by a third entry with Maserati power.

A driver line up including three times winner Henri Pescarolo reflected the seriousness of Ligier's '75 bid, even if it didn't have the speed of a pure prototype entry. Sadly two cars were eliminated by accidents but the third finished second, just one lap behind the winning Mirage. After that result the team went Grand Prix racing.

1976 saw the introduction of the Grand Touring Prototype (GTP) category which re-introduced pure coupe bodied prototypes in the form of the Inaltera/Rondeau and WM entries. The stories of these pioneers of Group C are detailed in the following section.

Aside from the French GTP cars, the 1978 winning Alpine Renault A442B almost qualified as a coupe. It was a spyder fitted with a hinged cockpit 'bubble' formed of clear perspex and in which there was a slot for improved forward vision and ventilation. The drivers complained of excessive cockpit heat but the aerodynamic benefit was such that the car was able to reach a speed of 217m.p.h. in qualifying. A similar canopy appeared on the bizzare Dome Zero cars run in '79, '80 and '81. Then came Group C and the mandatory return to proper coupe chassis...

Porsche had set a trend by running very successful spyders from the start of the '69 season: Alfa Romeo, Ferrari, Matra and others had followed suit for Group 6 which did not dictate a minimum windscreen height. In '72 3.0 litre Group 6 became the leading endurance class and the spyder style was run everywhere, even Le Mans. An open car had the advantage of better ventilation for the driver, better visibility and was less claustrophobic as well as being an obvious means of reducing weight and frontal area. A coupe body, however, promised less drag and better driver protection in inclement weather so there were a few coupe experiments at Le Mans during the lean spyder years of the Seventies.

In 1972 a privately entered but factory assisted Porsche 908 long tail coupe finished third overall at Le Mans, of course, and the weekend was also noteable for a new coupe design. This was, however, based on a productionised sports car, the Ligier, first seen at Le Mans in 1970 running a 1.8 litre Cosworth Ford FVC engine. Three Ligier JS2s appeared in 1972 fitted with race prepared versions of the SM Maserati V6 engine enlarged to 2991cc. and producing 270b.h.p. The backbone chassis, glass fibre bodied model was outclassed by the proper prototypes and all three cars retired with engine problems.

At the 1973 Test Weekend the Gulf Oil sponsored Mirage team (formed by ex-JWA personnel led by John Horsman) presented one of its Len Bailey designed aluminium monocoque M6 prototypes with a sleek coupe body. This was the first serious coupe experiment by one of the Group 6 spyder manufacturers. The enclosed Mirage M6 reflected traditional Le Mans aerodynamic theory having a lengthened tail section surmounted by a twin fin mounted rear aerofoil with surface fences.

The M6 coupe was designed to accept the 3.0 litre Weslake Ford V12 engine for which power was claimed to be 460b.h.p. at 10,600r.p.m. Alas, engine problems led to the team entering regular Cosworth propelled spyders for the race. However, the less fleet Ligier coupes re-appeared, again meeting with little in the way of success, an oil leak and an engine failure eliminating the two that were entered directly by the factory while the private entry came home 19th.

When two works JS2s appeared for the 1974 race the benefit of a full season of competition was obvious. The race prepared Maserati engine was now reputed to be producing 380b.h.p. at 8,400r.p.m. and both cars were among the top dozen qualifiers for the weakly supported event. In the race one car was eliminated by valve failure

TURBOS &
VENTURIS
1980 - 1988

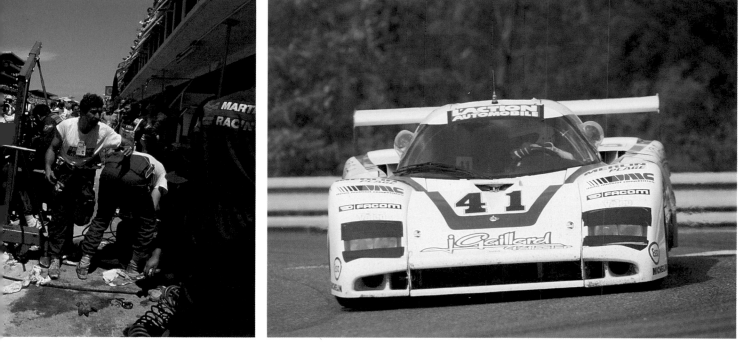

COLOUR PORTFOLIO
1980 - 1988

Page 89

Distinctive dorsum of the Sauber SHS C6 driven by Stuck/Schlesser/Quester in 1982. The car only lasted 76 laps, victim of Ford DFL vibration. Sauber would be back with BMW then Mercedes power...

Page 90

It looked as though it wasn't going to make it... The Holbert/Haywood/Schuppan works Porsche 956 lost its door near the end of the '83 race and disrupted airflow cooked its engine. It only just won!

Page 90

Private Porsches, works Lancia. The Brock/Perkins car carrying the hopes of Australian Porsche enthusiasts leads the similar 956 of Johansson/Schlesser/de Narvarez and a Lancia LC2 during the 1984 event.

Page 91

Night pits action as the Johansson/Schlesser/de Narvarez Joest Porsche 956 receives attention during the 1984 race. Johansson crashed the car on oil, ending its race, but the sister 956 entry of Pescarolo/Ludwig won.

Page 92-93

Heavy traffic during the 1985 race with Lancia, EMKA-Aston Martin and Jaguar interlopers among the Porsches. Jaguar had high hopes for its Group 44 challengers but even the EMKA-Aston Martin almost humbled it...

Page 94-95

Tribute to a great competitor. Jean-Louis Lafosse was one of the very best of French endurance racing drivers. Tragically, he lost his life in this Rondeau M379C when it crashed on the Mulsanne during the 1981 race.

Page 94

Eastern challenger: the Toyota propelled Dome of Elgh/Gabbiani/Suzuki in action during the 1986 race. The Japanese car had a 2.1 litre four cylinder engine with advanced engine management and a twin entry IHI turbocharger.

Page 94

Lancia had a golden opportunity in 1984 with the withdrawal of the Porsche works team. Its LC2 challengers were swift but yet again failed to last. Here the Wollek/Nannini example has its gearbox rebuilt.

Page 95

The Panic/Pessiot/Fornage WMP83B-Peugeot in action during the 1985 race. By the mid Eighties WM had lost all hope of outright victory against heavily funded works teams and subsequently turned to project 400k.p.h.

Page 96-97

The Raphanel/Regout/Courage Cougar C20 gets pits attention during the 1987 race. Note the Porsche flat six engine supplied to constructor Courage, a locally based Porsche dealer. The car finished a splendid third.

Page 98

Routine refuelling for the Guitteny/Yver/Sotty Rondeau M382 during the 1982 race. The 3.0 litre Cosworth DFV propelled car finished tenth just over 50 laps behind the winning Porsche 956. The DFV's day was over.

Page 98

The EMKA-Aston Martin appeared in 1983, driven by Needell/Faure/O'Rourke. The Len Bailey designed car badly lacked testing yet overcame a broken suspension and a holed radiator to finish.

Page 98-99

The Inaltera-Cosworth of Lombardi/Beckers/Ragnotti in full flight during the '77 race. The Inaltera was the first design of local constructor Jean Rondeau and was built for the GTP class from which Group C emerged.

Page 100

The Wollek/Schuppan/van der Merwe Porsche 962 in action during the 1988 race. The works-run car became the strongest challenger to the leading Jaguar until its Motronic M1.7 equipped engine broke just before 3.00am.

Page 102

The Raphanel/Regout/Courage Cougar-Porsche heads for third during the 1987 race. The locally built car gave the best performance for a French constructed car for many years as Courage tried to emulate Rondeau.

Page 103

The Baldi/Barilla/Heyer Lancia LC2 ran very strongly in 1984. The car featured a 3.0 litre engine rather than its regular 2.65 litre Ferrari V8 and was right in the spotlight until it broke fifth gear just after 4.00 am.

Page 102-103

Another shot of the fabulous EMKA-Aston Martin at Le Mans in 1983. The car had a ground effect underbody and carried its V8 engine more heavily stressed than the earlier Nimrod following work by Aston Martin Tickford on the sump.

Page 104

The Mallock/Olson Nimrod-Aston Martin was the fastest 'atmo' car in the 1984 race, comfortably out-qualifying the Jaguars. Alas, Olson crashed avoiding the sister car of Sheldon in a team wipe-out.

CHEETAH
ASTON MARTIN

Designed by Swiss race car builder Chuck Graemiger, the Cheetah G604 was the first composite chassis Group C1 car to appear at Le Mans, arriving in 1985. Its tub of carbon fibre and Kevlar was built by Advanced Composites of Derby while its stressed engine was the Tickford prepared Aston Martin V8 as used in the '83 EMKA.

The car's g.r.p. body bore resemblance to an earlier Cosworth DFL engined Cheetah that had been entered for Le Mans but had not appeared. It featured a front mounted water radiator and side mounted oil radiators. A nose splitter regulated the airflow to an underwing while a tail section reminiscent of a Porsche 956 was surmounted by a full width rear aerofoil.

The Cheetah qualified well back after numerous headaches and crashed when a hub failed in the seventh hour of the race.

CHEETAH	ASTON MARTIN
G604 - 1985	90 degree V8
Composite monocoque	5.3 litres
Suspension:	Alloy block
wishbone front	Fuel injected
rocker arm rear	16 valves
Engine stressed	d.o.h.c.
Hewland gearbox	Unblown
Ground effect car	580b.h.p.

EMKA ASTON MARTIN

The EMKA was built by Michael Cane for Steve O'Rourke. Its chassis was conceived by Len Bailey, who had been involved in the design of the original GT40. The chassis was a high sided aluminium monocoque with a forward footbox structure. The front suspension was of fabricated upper rocker arms with lower wishbones and inboard spring/dampers. At the rear were wide based lower wishbones with reversed upper wishbones and single trailing links with the spring/damper units situated either side of the bellhousing.

The single fuel cell was centrally mounted as required by Group C regulations. The bodywork was made from glassfibre reinforced plastic and was built by Protoco. A short, sharply inclined nose and long tail section gave the car a similar appearance in profile to Bailey's earlier Ford C100. The leading edge of the nose featured a blister like the tip of a single seater car nose cone which divided the air flowing under the car to the venturi tunnels. Water and oil radiators were side mounted with large NACA ducts cut into the flanks, the hot air venting through the upper surface of the tail ahead of the rear wheels. The engine was covered by a slatted rear window.

The 5340cc Aston Martin engine was similar to that used in the Nimrod cars in 1982 although a purpose-cast adaptor plate meant that the unit could now be fitted as a fully stressed member in the EMKA. Further Tickford refinements included new cylinder liners and valve gear with special attention paid to keeping the lower area of the engine from obstructing the underbody. A Hewland VG5 gearbox transmitted a quoted 580bhp at 7000rpm to the road. A wider power band was claimed, ranging between 5000 and 7000rpm, the Nimrods having had the range of only 5500 to 6500rpm.

The EMKA was run at the 1983 Silverstone 1000 kilometres as a dress rehearsal for Le Mans and broke down on the last lap when a hub seized. At Le Mans Needell qualified it 26th having reached 209mph on the straight. Co-Driven by Faure and owner O'Rourke the car suffered a holed radiator and needed repairs to the rear suspension but managed to finish 17th.

A lack of sponsorship meant that the EMKA was unused for the entire 1984 season but towards the end of that year Dow Corning announced sponsorship for an attempt at the 1985 Le Mans race. The car was subjected to an aerodynamic development program by Richard Owen who had designed successful cars for the Sports 2000 club racing category. The ground effect underbody was removed with a consequent weight saving and the rear aerofoil was raised up into the airstream on twin vertical fins. A conventional-type air splitter now formed the leading edge of the nose. The side radiator vents in the rear deck were closed off, hot air now exiting through the open bottom of the car. Under the skin new uprights and hubs had been fitted after the failures in previous races. The Silverstone race was used again in preparation for Le Mans, the EMKA using a nose mounted aerofoil to balance the rear wing here.

At Le Mans Needell lapped the revised car nine seconds quicker than on its' previous visit to line up 13th on the grid. The deletion of the ground effect had eliminated the drag penalty such cars usually suffered on the long straight. In the race the revitalised car lead briefly in the opening stages due to an early refuelling stop which put it out of schedule with the leading runners. By the end of the race a reliable run had brought it home in 11th place.

EMKA	ASTON MARTIN
83C - 1983	90 degree V8
Alloy monocoque	5.3 litres
Suspension:	Alloy block
rocker arm front	Fuel injected
rocker arm rear	16 valves
Engine stressed	d.o.h.c.
Hewland gearbox	Unblown
Ground effect car	580b.h.p.

NIMROD ASTON MARTIN

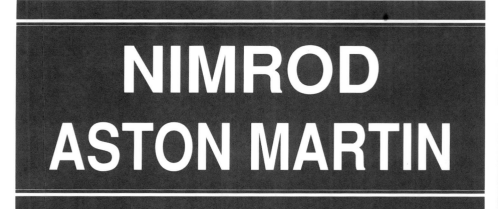

Nimrod Racing Automobiles was formed in 1981 by Robin Hamilton and Victor Gauntlett.

The first Nimrod rolling chassis was built to IMSA specification as no finalised Group C regulations were available. The slab sided aluminium monocoque was to an Eric Broadley design having much in common with the Lola T70. Suspension was conventional with many components being incorporated from the current Lola Indy Car project.

The Aston Martin V8 engine was directly descended from that used in the 1967 Lola Le Mans car, now reputedly producing 580 bhp at 7250 rpm. A Group C Nimrod was completed in time for a debut at the Silverstone 1000 kms. This car was similar to the IMSA chassis but had the single central fuel tank required under Group C regulations.

At Le Mans two cars were run, one by the factory and a second by Viscount Downe. The Downe car was two seconds faster in practice lining up 23rd on the grid with the works car three places behind. Alas, 3½ hours into the race a tyre failure pitched the factory entry backwards into the barriers on the Mulsanne straight when Needell was driving. That put the car, which had been running in tenth place, firmly out of the race.

The private entry was more fortunate and by the ninth hour it was running in sixth place. It moved up to fourth at half distance. A misfire on Sunday morning, indicating valve trouble, reduced the car to running on seven cylinders, trailing oil smoke. Despite stopping on the circuit with no fuel pressure, with 2½ hours remaining the car was revived and it was nursed to a seventh place finish by Mallock/Phillips/Salmon.

Ambitious plans for 1983, centred around a new works chassis design by Andrew Thorby, but failed to materialise. Meanwhile the Downe car had been extensively modified by Ray Mallock. A new body shape doubled the downforce of the original car. Modifications to the chassis, suspension

and cooling systems were also evident with a 90 kgs weight saving.

At Le Mans a multitude of problems afflicted it early on; the alternator, brakes, gearbox and a fuel leak, only for a connecting rod to break with seven hours left to run.

By 1984 the original Nimrod Racing Automobiles company had failed and Aston Martin had found new American owners who gave works backing to the Downe team. In an air of optimism a lightweight chassis fitted with a newly developed twin turbocharged Tickford Aston Martin engine was debuted at Silverstone. The engine showed promise but was considered too new for Le Mans. The lightweight car was consequently run in normally aspirated form for Mallock/Olson with the older, heavier car for Salmon/Attwood/Sheldon.

The lighter Nimrod (which featured titanium springs and carbon fibre bodywork) was faster than the American entered Jaguars in practice. In the race Mallock/Olson had moved into the top 10 by the third hour before things went disastrously wrong. Around 9.15 on the Saturday evening the team's second car with Sheldon driving crashed heavily at the Mulsanne kink killing a track marshal. The driver was burnt but managed to escape. Olson had been following closely, hit debris from the accident and spun into the barriers. One car was damaged and one was destroyed; along with it went the spirit of the project. Finances already at full stretch, the Nimrods were never raced again and the turbocharged Aston Martin engine was shelved.

NIMROD	ASTON MARTIN
GpC - 1982	90 degree V8
Alloy monocoque	5.3 litres
Suspension:	Alloy block
rocker arm front	Fuel injected
wishbone rear	16 valves
Engine semi-stressed	d.o.h.c.
Hewland gearbox	Unblown
Flat bottom	

ROADE WORKS

Aston Martin had high hopes for its Nimrod project. Alas, the car was under powered, overweight and suffered poor aerodynamics. Driver/engineer Ray Mallock took a privately owned example by the scruff of the neck and made a racing car out of it. Ian Bamsey asked Mallock how he went about the creation of the Aston Martin Downe.

Having dominated the 1981 British Formula Atlantic Championship, 30 year old Ray Mallock found himself at what he describes as "a crossroads" in his career. Returning from Macau (where he finished the classic street race in a fine third place) he read about Aston Martin's return to international racing with the Nimrod project.

Nimrod Racing was set up by long time Aston Martin racing enthusiast Robin Hamilton together with Aston Martin's executive chairman Victor Gauntlett and its American distributor Peter Livanos. The company's aim was to race a car in the new Group C World Endurance Championship using a 5.3 litre Aston Martin V8 engine supplied by the factory and developed on its behalf by Aston Martin Tickford. The chassis was based on tub and running gear designed and produced by Lola Cars with bodywork shaped and produced by Nimrod.

Mallock had worked at Aston Martin as an apprentice and maintained close links through driving works entered V8 Vantage development cars in British club racing events. The concept of sportscar racing appealed to him and an initial approach led to a certain amount of testing work in the prototype Nimrod-Aston Martin over the '81/82 off-season period.

At this stage Viscount Downe struck a deal to purchase his own car from Nimrod to be run by Richard Williams from the Brixton workshop in which many DB series cars were prepared by Williams for historic racing. Mallock knew Williams well having raced a Williams-prepared Lola Group 6 spyder at Le Mans in '79 and this led to him becoming drawn into the Downe project. With hindsight, that was crucial since it gave him the opportunity to guide development and engineering in a way that would never have been possible had he joined the works driving strength.

Mallock had his own team, Ray Mallock Racing, which had run his Atlantic car and also did race preparation and track testing for a variety of customers from its Roade, near Silverstone, base. Mallock's chief mechanic Willem Toet and an assistant went down to Brixton to help prepare the car and attended test sessions and race meetings.

The first test was at Silverstone early in '82 and straight out of the box the Downe car (chassis 003) beat the works testing times. Mallock admits there was always plenty of friendly rivalry and he was naturally keen to beat the likes of works drivers Needell and Lees. Mallock was a gifted test driver with a solid knowledge of racing car engineering and as a result of his experience with the works prototype he had advised different rear wing flaps and springs for the Brixton-

Support from the Bovis construction group helped Mallock and Richard Williams keep Viscount Downe's modified Nimrod on the track in 1984.

oprepared machine. He says that generally the 1015kg car was very controllable and very enjoyable to drive, "although, you were aware of the weight".

Nimrod's testing had shown that the V8 was liable to run hot and was prone to break valve springs. With two valves per cylinder it had relatively big, heavy valves and the valve problem would eventually see the Aston Martin race engine developed for the late Eighties adopt new four valve heads, for more controllable smaller, lighter valves with less inertia. In the light of the problems Williams imposed a 6,500rpm rev limit for the season whereas the works cars were run to 7,200rpm.

An early chassis modification was the installation of a revised swirl pot and header tank since Mallock and Williams considered the original system was not de-aerating properly, contributing to the high water temperature. The Nimrod chassis was a classic aluminium monocoque car derived from Lola's T70 design of the Sixties and even retained a T70 windscreen and pedal bracket. Of course, it was far from an update of the T70 and, for example, employed uprights from a contemporary (late Seventies) Lola Indy car and it had rocker arm front suspension. Mallock could see no logic in the rocker arm layout which added extra weight and complexity and the whole car was badly overweight at 1015kg (compared to an 800kg weight limit) with its alloy engine and heavy duty Hewland VGC gearbox installed. The car was ruggedly built from well proven components but its chassis weight had not necessarily been put to the best use and over 200 excess

kilos was a major drawback, particularly as the engine produced less than 550bhp.

The Nimrod was a flat bottom car and had been designed specifically for low drag with Le Mans its primary target. Its Hamilton-designed bodywork was slippery but left the car woefully short of downforce. For the Silvestone 1000kms race debut Mallock devised an alternative wing for the Downe car and modified the nose with a new-style, more effective splitter and an extractor lip across the front of the radiator outlet which offered a useful gain in downforce at little if any drag penalty. Further, the extractor flap helped draw air from the radiator, assisting cooling. In addition, the front suspension geometry was altered for improved turn in at the advice of Arthur Mallock Senior.

In spite of running only 6,500rpm the modified Downe Nimrod qualified faster than the works car and, unlike its sister car, it made it home, in a solid sixth position. Thereafter the car and the team's one engine were rebuilt ready for Le Mans, for which the Silverstone configuration was retained. Henceforth both this and the works car had to be fitted with 'taxi signs' atop the cockpit since the T70 windscreen had been set too low: the Nimrod's height did not conform to the Group C minimum.

Le Mans brought further encouragement, though the car clearly lacked power badly: Porsche was running its new Porsche 956 at 800kg. and could turn up its boost to give over 600bhp in spite of the fuel restrictions. With its extra downforce and lower revs, the Downe car was found to lack 15 - 20mph compared to the speed of the works car on the Mulsanne but over the complete lap its

Full bore at Le Mans in 1984 - The highly competitive Mallock/Olson Nimrod from which much was expected. Alas, it went so badly wrong...

superior grip paid dividends: Mallock/Salmon/Phillips qualified almost two seconds faster than Needell/Lees/Evans (who were running the same tyres).

The works car crashed following tyre failure in the race while the Downe car ran like a steamtrain until only the works Porsches were ahead. Only two of three works Porsches survived in good health so the private Nimrod was on course for third when, at around threequarter distance, brake discs started to crack. With its weight and lack of ground effect the car was heavy on its brakes (conventional cast iron discs with four pot calipers from AP) and Le Mans is notorious for cracked discs due to the thermal shock as brakes cool on the Mulsanne then are banged on as hard as possible for the sharp Mulsanne corner.

At least two disc changes were required, then the engine started to cough. An electrical problem was suspected as it lapsed onto seven cylinders but it later transpired to be a burning away of valve seats, probably caused by the Lucas mechanically-injected V8 running too lean in the cool of the night. Running on progressively fewer cylinders, the car was nursed home into seventh place. It crawled in to accept the accolade of highest placed British car.

Le Mans was round four of the World Endurance Championship for Makes and the fifth and final round was the Spa 1000km in September. Running again in 'Silverstone' configuration and with its

regular engine, the Downe car again made the top ten, scoring sufficient points to give Aston Martin third in the Makes title chase. While Downe could count two dozen points, Nimrod Racing could count a dozen engines failures...

Brands Hatch was next on the Downe calendar and since drag was of little importance at the sinuous Kent circuit Mallock conceived the concept of a front wing, to be mounted above the splitter. He borrowed a wing from a Mallock clubmans car and fabricated the necessary supports for the full width appendage. The concept was revived a few years later by Porsche Group C and GTP racers. It was balanced at the rear by a steeper wing angle.

Again the Downe car was quicker than the works car and Mallock had plans to make it quicker still since, unlike Nimrod Racing, Viscount Downe could not aspire to construct a new car for the following season. As early as Le Mans Mallock had put forward a proposal to radically modify the machine, lightening and improving its aerodynamics as far as realistic budgetary considerations would allow. In any case the cockpit shape would have to be modified to bring the car more cleanly to the regulation height.

Mallock got the go-ahead to lighten the car as far as possible short of a costly re-engineering of the dated chassis and to produce a entirely new bodyshape. Consequently, the car was stripped down at Roade where Mallock and his lads went through it from stem to stern, looking for every last ounce. There were other improvements, too. The new dash layout was tidier. The revised brake ducting was more efficient. The pontoon mounted oil tank was changed for an engine bay tank which was taller and more efficient as well as lighter, and helped reduce cockpit temperatures. The new rear suspension mount was more rigid as well as lighter. This and neater

front and rear subframes were designs detailed by freelance designer Graham Humphries. Mallock would have liked to have produced a lighter outboard front suspension but didn't have the budget for major alterations of that nature.

In the area of aerodynamics Mallock called on the advice of a number of friends, including Alan Jenkins of McLaren and Ron Tauranac. The new body had, of course, to fit the existing running gear and that ruled out the possibility of full ground effects since there was no room under the engine bay for a diffuser upsweep. However, the car, still woefully short of power, was in any case to remain a Le Mans special. Mallock had the budget to produce a new windscreen and came up with a sleeker shape (as narrow overall as possible given the constraints of front wheel movement) of which a one quarter scale model was made for wind tunnel testing.

The wooden model was evaluated in the fixed floor tunnel at MIRA, Mallock having the benefit of the lift and drag figures for the tunnel testing of the original shape at MIRA. The key gains sought were more downforce without drag penalty and improved cooling and improved ducting to the airbox since it was suspected that the original design lacked pressure in its airbox which was fed from a NACA duct in each flank.

A lot of work was done detailing the nose shape and splitter and the sides of the splitter, immediately ahead of each front wheel, were made to lead, under the nose, into a venturi. Thus air was accelerated under the splitter then was diffused into the wheel arch. It was found that setting a vertical air exit slot into the car's flank just behind the wheel arch helped draw air through the venturi. Various options were investigated for the visible nose shape but here it was found that downforce gains were at the penalty of too much drag.

However, both top and bottom nose surfaces were reprofiled.

At the rear, a long tail was found beneficial for drag reduction and since there was not the budget for both long and short tails this was standardized. However, fast and slow circuit wing and spoiler options were identified. For Le Mans, the wing was mounted high in the airstream and thus was working very efficiently and could be flattened right off. It was run with a low tail spoiler. For other tracks, increasing the wing's angle of attack increased rear downforce but had a cantilever effect, pitching the car so that the nose lifted. Thus, the wing had to be lowered. However, the spoiler height could be raised since this was found to increase downforce over the entire car.

Another detail at the rear was an inner wheel arch carefully profiled to follow the tyre as closely as possible. A tyre acts as an air pump: reducing the volume of air whipped around by tyre rotation reduced drag. The net result of the work at MIRA was a drag co-efficient equal to that of the original Nimrod (0.38) with no less than three times the downforce - a worthwhile achievement. From less than 1, the lift to drag ratio became 2:1.

Not only was the new shape (with all leading edges rounded off) detailed at MIRA, it was pressure plotted to identify the best position for inlet ducting. The main aim was find an improved feed for the engine and this took the form of twin NACA ducts set into the roof, just ahead of the airbox. The inlets for radiator and front brake cooling were incorporated in a single slot above the splitter to reduce the overall number of ducts.

The buck for the Downe body was built by Alan Fenn and was transferred into g.r.p.

(anything more exotic would have been too costly) at his Tunbridge Wells 'shop. The so-called Aston Martin Downe rolled out of Mallock's workshop at around 950kg. It was ready for testing just before the '83 Silverstone 1000km. Running in low steep wing/high spoiler trim it immediately showed a gain of three seconds per lap. The only problem was that a new combined water/oil radiator was found to be marginal and this was replaced by twin oil radiators riding piggy back on a wider water radiator.

After the shakedown the car was again based in Brixton, from where it was run in the Silverstone 1000kms, finishing seventh, then the Le Mans 24 hour race. At Le Mans speed on the Mulsanne was up from 200mph to 214mph and this was attributed to the new air box intake, which offered the additional bonus that air no longer passed through the oil radiator en route to the engine. Over the complete lap, mainly due to the additional downforce, the car was no less than 11 seconds quicker. It couldn't hope to challenge the Porsche 956 for sheer speed due to its relative lack of power but reliability ought to have been its trump card. Alas, a broken oil line caused eventual engine failure during the race.

That was a major disappointment after working sixth months to engineer a vastly improved car and looking strong on the day, Mallock recalls: "I felt that our Le Mans potential had been high, but that it had been unfulfilled".

Following non-points scoring forays to Spa and Brands Hatch the car went under a dust cover. However, Mallock was keen to take it to Daytona, reckoning that in the high speed, partially banked circuit's 24 hour race it could prove its worth. A deal came together involving Drake Olson and John Sheldon as co-drivers and Williams was able to ship out the car complete with a spare engine on this occasion.

The Aston Martin Downe went well at Daytona, only for wheel bearings to check progress in the race. A lot of time was lost as all four corners went at some stage or other. The ball bearings incorporated in the Indy car uprights clearly weren't adequate given the loads imposed by the 950kg. machine on the banking and subsequently taper bearings were installed.

While it had been running the modified Nimrod had gone well against the Group 44 Jaguars. It had less power but less drag and "seemed better balanced, able to go through the corners more consistently", Mallock reckons. The fact that the car could match Jaguar pace impressed Livanos and he helped fund the '84 European effort and bought a second chassis, Nimrod 005, which had been run at Daytona by owner John Cooper.

Mallock's quarter scale wooden model undergoes evaluation in the MIRA fixed floor wind tunnel. Work here led to a vastly improved car shape.

At Roade 005 was converted to Aston Martin Downe specification but halfway through the work Tickford offered a turbocharged engine. Clearly, power was lacking from the normally aspirated engine which Mallock rates at around 520bhp. The lightly boosted Tickford twin turbo V8 was reckoned to offer up to 700bhp but required a huge amount of work to install, complete with air:air aftercoolers. Testing commenced at Silverstone then continued at Snetterton and the GM Millbrook proving ground where a lap at an average speed of over 200mph was acheived, likely for the first time ever anywhere in the UK!

Alas, that was the turbocar's claim to fame since the engine didn't offer significantly increased performance and was unreliable. It raced once, at Silverstone, where the head gasket failed early on. Mallock recalls: "testing continued after Silverstone but we had a lot of engine problems. We never got the performance and it never held together. One week before Le Mans the decision was taken to run two normally aspirated cars there..."

The two Aston Martin Downes, running essentially to '83 specification, arrived at Le Mans as works entries thanks to the Livanos connection. As a result there were qualifying tyres and there was even a qualifying engine. This was to the regular race engine specification but since it was not to be raced the team was happy to run it to 7,200rpm. The result was a gain of another two seconds and tenth quickest time for Mallock/Olson, ahead of all the other atmo cars and over two seconds quicker than the best Jaguar could manage.

"We were very pleased with the car's performance...", Mallock recalls, "and the race started smoothly. We were getting along nicely when the accident happened..."

Alas, this was the incident that shattered the project. Sheldon lost control of 003 in the kink. Either a tyre blew out or a slow puncture took its toll. A tyre that has lost pressure tends to be kept on the rim by centrifugal force on the straight, only to collapse once cornering loads are put through it. 003 went over the barrier into the trees, debris killing a marshal though Sheldon somehow survived, badly burned. Olson arrived as Sheldon's car was an airborne fireball. He braked, couldn't see the track in the dust and spun into the barrier, smashing the front of the car.

That was the end of the team. 005 was rebuilt for Livanos' collection in the autumn while a few years later Mallock made a new tub around which 003 was revived for Downe's collection. At around the same time he was busy building a chassis for the exciting four valve Aston Martin engine, schedule to race in 1989...

URD & SAUBER BMW

At Le Mans in 1982 a stubby little red coupe powered by a 3.5 litre BMW M1 straight six engine appeared. Its URD C81 chassis had originally been commissioned by Jurgen Kannacher for use in the German sports car championship and it was designed and built by Ernst Ungar's URD Rennwagenbau in Germany. Only one of three space frame designs to compete in Group C, it was a very simple flat bottom design with conventional suspension, outboard brakes and a nose mounted radiator. The angular g.r.p. bodywork had gull wing doors and was distinguished by a rear wing mounted on fins that overhung the short tail.

The production based engine prepared by Weigel RennTechnik produced 450bhp for the race, though a more powerful Schnitzer engine was fitted for qualifying. The car qualified half way down the grid and was an early retirement with engine failure. A year later, in new hands, the car finished 14th. In subsequent years the URD-BMW became a C2 regular, the engine woefully short of power by C1 standards.

Nevertheless, Sauber managed a top 10 finish running a BMW M1 engine in 1983. The Sauber C7 was a new prototype chassis equipped with a Mader prepared version of the engine rated at 460bhp. The chassis was an aluminium sheet monocoque with side mounted radiators and traditional suspension. The bodywork featured a large cutaway in the lower nose to feed a ground effect underbody. A conventional centre post rear aerofoil was run. In spite of its relative lack of power the Swiss-built car hit 200mph and it was driven by an IMSA crew to a ninth place finish thanks to a faultless run, stopping a Porsche clean sweep of the top 10 places. Subsequently Sauber switched to more powerful engines.

SAUBER	BMW
C7 - 1983	in line 6
Alloy monocoque	3.5 litres
Suspension:	Iron block
wishbone front	Fuel injected
wishbone rear	24 valves
Engine semi-stressed	d.o.h.c.
Hewland gearbox	Unblown
Ground effect car	460b.h.p.

MARCH 82/84G BUICK & CHEVROLET

Designed by Robin Herd, the March 82G had an aluminium honeycomb monocoque with conventional suspension and four pot, single caliper brakes from AP. The body shape and underwing profile were based on knowledge gained from the design and construction of the BMW M1C IMSA GTP car that March had produced in 1981. Again, Max Sardou was aerodynamic consultant and the carbon fibre/Kevlar body set a water radiator and an aerofoil between twin nose booms. Sardou claimed that his clean 82G shape had 20% less drag than the M1C with no loss of downforce.

The 82G ran mainly in IMSA GTP as a customer car with Chevrolet power at 900kg. but the factory supported a two car Le Mans effort. A Garretson Enterprises car had a Lucas injected, Woods built 5811cc Chevrolet V8 rated 600 bhp while a March Racing chassis ran a 5835cc Weiss Chevrolet with Bosch injection and a claimed 580 bhp. Both rumbling heavyweights qualified well down the grid. The factory car retired after seven hours with electrical failure while the Garretson car ran out of fuel during the third hour.

The 82G chassis subsequently developed through the 83G to the 84G finding much IMSA success along the way. An 84G appeared at Le Mans in 1984 equipped with a 3.4 litre Buick V6 turbo engine prepared by McLaren Engines of Detroit. It was second fastest on the Mulsanne at 222 mph in qualifying but was slow over the entire lap and the engine blew during the tenth hour of the race.

MARCH	CHEVROLET
82G - 1982	90 degree V8
Honeycomb monocoque	5.8 litres
Suspension:	Iron block
wishbone front	Fuel injected
wishbone rear	16 valves
Engine semi stressed	Pushrod
Hewland gearbox	Unblown
Ground effect car	600b.h.p.

RONDEAU
3 SERIES PRE'81
COSWORTH

In 1980 Jean Rondeau became the first man in history to win the Le Mans 24 Hour race in a car of his own manufacture. The forerunners of this car were first seen at the 1976 race when two GRP bodied, aluminium monocoque chassis powered by Ford DFV engines producing 415 bhp at 9500 rpm were raced by Pescarolo/Beltoise and Rondeau/Jaussaud/Beckeers. The cars, named Inalteras in deference to their wallpaper and paint manufacturing sponsor, both finished, the lead car eighth, its team mate 21st.

In 1977 the Inaltera team ran at the Daytona 24 hours in preparation for Le Mans, at which three cars were entered, two cars running in the Group 6 sports prototype class, one in GTP. Once again all the cars finished, the GTP chassis fourth overall, winning its class, driven by Rondeau/Ragnotti. The Group 6 cars finished 11th and 13th for Beckers/Lombardi and Beltoise/Holbert.

The 1978 race saw the debut of the Rondeau M378, a development of the Inaltera. Engine and chassis were similar to the previous car but bodywork changes included a longer finned tail which partially covered the rear wheels. The new car was entered in the GTP class with one of the Inalteras now owned by Swiss Andre Chevalley as on of its rivals. The older car was faster in practice but by the end of the race the M378 of Rondeau/Darniche/Haren was ninth overall and won the class again. The Inaltera was thirteenth driven by its owner and Trisconi and Rondeau's 100% finishing record was maintained.

Three cars were entered for the 1979 race, two in Group 6, a third trying to maintain dominance of the GTP class. Bodywork and suspension changes had been made to the design which was now running as the M379 and was fitted with Heini Mader prepared DFV engines. The

Group 6 class and fifth overall went to rally drivers Darniche/Ragnotti with ex-F1 men Pescarolo/Beltoise second in class and tenth overall. The GTP car blotted the marque's copybook by registering its first retirement in four years of Le Mans competition.

The M379 was uprated B specification for the 1980 race, with revisions made to internal air flow and cooling. Two narrow aerofoils were mounted each side between pairs of vertical fins atop a lengthened tail section. Mader tuned DFVs were used again with three cars entered, two in Group Six, one in GTP. Pescarolo/Ragnotti in one of the former disputed the lead with the Porsche favourite in the wet early stages before moving ahead at around quarter distance. The sister Group Six car climbed into second place soon after.

By the ten hour mark Pescarolo had retired with a blown head gasket leaving Rondeau/Jaussaud to challenge the Porsche that was now leading. With six hours remaining the German car ran into trouble. Despite pressure from the repaired Porsche the M379B held on to win and Jean Rondeau was a national hero. Almost forgotten in the hysteria, the GTP class had again been won by Rondeau, the car of Spice and the brothers Martin finishing third overall.

RONDEAU	COSWORTH
3 series - 1980	90 degree V8
Alloy monocoque	3.0 litres
Suspension:	Alloy block
wishbone front	Fuel injected
wishbone rear	32 valves
Engine stressed	d.o.h.c.
Hewland gearbox	Unblown
Flat bottom	480b.h.p.

MISSION IMPOSSIBLE

Jean Rondeau lived in Le Mans and became ensnared by the lure of its 24 hour race. He set about building his own car, having failed to find a potential winning drive. On paper, his mission was at best optimistic. But somehow Rondeau managed the seemingly impossible. Ian Bamsey asked Philippe Beloou, Technical Director in 1980, how it was done.

Jean Rondeau lived in Le Mans. He had the 24 Hour race in his blood. A club racing driver, he got a Le Mans ride in a humble Mazda in '75 and vowed to build his own car to win. Consequently, the ambitious 31 year old formed a team, A.T.A.C. (Association pour la vulgarisation et la promotion des techniques de courses automobiles) with some friends. They and set about the design of a car to conform to the GTP class the ACO had just announced for the 1976 running of its classic.

GTP called for a full height windscreen, token baggage space and a higher minimum weight than the regular spyder-bodied prototypes while aiming to attract a variety of engine solutions: only a maximum consumption of 35 litres per 100km. was specified. Rondeau envisaged use of the Peugeot V6 engine and designed a coupe

shape with the help of Robert Choulet who ran the Eifel fixed floor wind tunnel. Choulet had previously worked with Porsche (on the 917LH) and Matra. By the autumn Rondeau had a proposed body shape which he was able to paint in Inaltera colours.

One time amateur racer Charles James ran the Inaltera decorating materials company and he still had big ambitions in racing. He agreed to fund the proposed GTP car providing it was known as an Inaltera and was Cosworth DFV propelled. A workshop was rented in Le Mans' Rue Hoche (no. 100) and eight young assistants were employed under Rondeau and Vic Elford who was appointed Team Manager, leaving the founder to concentrate on the technical side. All eight assistants spent the last quarter of '75 helping with the design: Hubert Rohee was chief draughtsman;

Daniel Menage was the chassis specialist while Jacques Besneville and Jean Philippe Desmottes concentrated on the bodywork. The other four mechanics were Philippe Beloou, Philippe Bone, Lucian Monte and Jean-Pierre Devaux.

Construction of the Inaltera began at the start of '76. It was a straightforward design with a plated spaceframe (Sixties Ferrari style) as the team lacked experience of monocoques and the GTP stipulations discouraged a traditional monocoque tub by excluding pannier tanks and limiting pannier width to 230mm. The chassis ended at the firewall bulkhead: the engine was fully stressed with the rear suspension hung from the transaxle. Twin water radiators were set into the firewall bulkhead, one either side of the cockpit, and the fuel tank was also centrally positioned (behind the seats) so the location of the centre of gravity would be unaffected as its 160 load diminished.

The straightforward spaceframe was produced in house from steel tubing and aluminium panelling. The suspension was of the classic outboard type with coil springs over Koni dampers. The Michelin shod car ran on Gotti 13" diameter magnesium/aluminium three piece wheels (front and rear wheels had to be the same diameter) and was stopped by 10" diameter AP discs grabbed by AP four pot calipers. The rear brakes were inboard, as was common in Formula One, to save unsprung weight. The transmission was a Hewland TL200 five speeder as used by Ligier in Formula One, running a cam and pawl differential and fed through an AP triple plate clutch.

From small acorns... The Rondeau campaign began with backing from Inaltera, after which the local team's first cars were named. This is the 1976 Inaltera-Cosworth GTP.

The clean-shaped fully enclosed body (conforming to the minimum overall height of 1100mm) sported only a small engine oil radiator in the nose as the water radiators fed through side ducts flanking the cockpit area. The body was of g.r.p. with Marchal lights, while Smiths supplied the instruments. The radiators (including one at the back for the gearbox) were from Sofica, while the fuel cell was from Superflexit. A 15 litre oil tank was carried in the engine bay.

The Inaltera came out at almost 900kg whereas GTP regulations allowed an 850kg minimum. However, it was designed primarily to be robust. By the mid Seventies Mirage had shown that the combination of Cosworth DFV engine and Hewland gearbox could last 24 hours and (in the absence of Matra) win. Neither the engine nor the gearbox manufacturer had planned to join the marathon running game but both had responded positively to the needs of teams such as Mirage. Cosworth had developed an 'endurance' DFV with reduced compression ratio, softer cams and a more conservative rev limit. Revving to 10,000rpm it produced around 420bhp. The Inaltera team bought three such engines and set about the construction of two additional chassis prior to the 1976 24 hour race.

The first Inaltera chassis made its debut at the private Bardinon circuit in the spring of '76. Henri Pescarolo and Jean-Pierre Beltoise both drove it over the course of a number of days and found it "quite correct", Beloou recalls. No fundamental modification was required and further tests were carried out at Paul Ricard then, for the two chassis to be run at La Sarthe, at the Michelin test track three weeks prior to the race.

It was a dream debut, both cars finishing with Pescarolo/Beltoise winning the GTP class in eighth overall while Rondeau/Jean-Pierre Jaussaud/"Christine" (Elford's companion) ran home 21st. Broken dampers were among the delays and the team subsequently switched to Bilstein.

Devaux left the Inaltera team after the race to join Ligier but otherwise it remained intact and at the request of James it sent two chassis to the Daytona 24 Hours in February 1977 where, alas, both retired. The cars ran on Goodyear in Florida and the team decided to stay with the American crossplies. For its second Le Mans assault all three cars were prepared with the same three engines as used in '76, and one entry ran in Group 6 without ballast. In the course of rebuilding weight had been saved, notably through lighter tubing and thinner body panels. The basic weight was now a respectable 820kg. The three engines were run in 480bhp "Formula One" trim and Mulsanne speed went up from 300 to 320kph.

Again the team recorded a 100% finishing record, Rondeau/Ragnotti winning GTP with a splendid fourth overall (only losing

third in the final hour). And on that high note the Inaltera adventure abruptly ended. Charles James had parted ways with the firm and as a direct consequence its racing team was disbanded. Everyone was laid off and the equipment was sold, lock, stock and barrel, to Heini Mader.

Rondeau didn't give up hope. A Tyrrell-influenced six wheeler project for '78 had to be shelved but he did manage to find a small amount of money enabling construction of the first 'Rondeau' chassis to begin in January '78. The backing was secured with the help of Marjorie Brosse (wife of the Prefect of La Sarthe) who had acted as the team's PR since early in '77 and was from the SKF, Facom and Marchal companies. In addition, the town of Le Mans lent an old workshop on the Montehard industrial estate.

The first Rondeau was built with the former Inaltera personnel working their evenings and weekends. It was very close to the original Inaltera design but with "evolutionary" changes throughout. The basic

body shape went unchanged: there were no funds for wind tunnel work and the old g.r.p. master was used once more. On the chassis, machined rather than welded parts saw a certain amount of weight saved: 760kg was now the unballasted figure. The basic specification was otherwise almost identical to that of the earlier cars. One brand new engine was bought from Cosworth while one ex-Inaltera engine was bought from Mader as a spare.

The Rondeau 'M378' was finished just in time for a day's shakedown on the Le Mans Bugatti circuit prior to the race where no major problem arose. The team now had a few full time employees: Bone, Desmottes, Rohee and Thibault, a newcomer experienced in chassis and suspension construction, though Elford was no longer associated with it. The new car was run for Rondeau and Bernard Darniche who

The car of Rondeau/Jaussaud at Le Mans in 1980 on a routine pit stop. It ran through to the finish without major setback and made its constructor a national hero

experienced few problems other than a broken gear shift linkage once rear body rigidity had been attended to in qualifying. Again Mulsanne speed was in the region of 320kph and yet again the local team claimed the GTP prize, ninth overall this year.

After the race the team rebuilt the car, tested it at Bugatti then closed the doors of the borrowed workshop while more money was sought. Nothing further happened until January 1979 when major backing from ITT was confirmed. Later VSD and Merlin Plage also came in. Rondeau moved his base to Champagne, 10km. from the town, and took on faithful helpers Beloou, Monte, Besneville and Menage full time once more. Henceforth Rondeau concentrated on administration and Beloou became Technical Director. Two more chassis were constructed and, according to Beloou, "for the first time our aim was to win outright".

There was no fundamental difference between the rebuilt M378 and the two new M379s. The M378 had an improved gear linkage and similar modifications where appropriate to assist the all important quest for reliability. There was also a reprofiling of the nose to decrease downforce: the '78 car had too much downforce at the front following a subtle redesign of its nose from the Inaltera shape. The new cars were to the same design but without ballast to run in Group 6 in the search for outright winning pace. The team had looked at the possibility of removing the windscreen and cockpit canopy but concluded that a complete redesign was called for and that was beyond its financial means.

The '79 trio was completed just before the race, again allowing only a little time for testing on the Bugatti circuit. The lead Group 6 car for Pecarolo/Beltoise was tried with modified front suspension geometry as the small wheel diameter had led to slow corner oversteer in the past but the experiment (shifting the front roll centre) was not a success. Again 480bhp engines were run to 10,000rpm (9,800rpm on the Mulsanne) and again the top speed was in the region of 320kph. The team only had three engines, all Mader prepared. In the absence of Renault, it was allocated the prime paddock position.

Rondeau shared the GTP car with old friend Jacky Haran. In the wet Haran aquaplaned off the circuit and hit the guardrail. The impact broke the chassis: the first retirement in nine starts. However, both Group 6 cars came home, overcoming problems with the gear linkage, cracked rod ends and troublesome wets that rapidly chunked. Ragnotti/Darniche won Group 6 with fifth overall while Pescarolo/Beltoise ran home tenth overall.

July '79 found the team without finance once again. However, outside engineering contracts kept it in business and one of the two surviving Group 6 cars was modified in response to the problems incurred during the race. Alterations included small winglets at the rear as rear end downforce had been found wanting and Gurney flaps had added too much drag. By January 1980 some backing had been found and the modified car was tested over 26 hours at Paul Ricard. This was the first real test for the M378/379 design away from the race. The only problem that occurred was a broken finger in the gearbox: "we were sure now the car was as reliable as possible" says Beloou.

Three cars were again prepared, with support from Le Point and renewed backing

Inaltera GTP, 1976 style. The Cosworth engine nestles in a tube-frame based sports-prototype chassis, unusual at this time not only for its construction but also for its coupe body.

from ITT, all to the 'M379B' (Ricard) specification, again weighing around 760kg without ballast. Two chassis were the '79 Group 6 machines updated, the third was new. The same three engines were run (the team still having no spare) and again one example was run in GTP (a new car ballasted by heavyweight body panels), two in Group 6.

The GTP entry was backed by Belga and was crewed by Gordon Spice and the Martin brothers and yet again the team won the category, finishing a splendid third overall. However, in Group 6 it suffered its first retirement due to mechanical failure, its Pescarolo/Ragnotti car (which had won pole) cracking a cylinder overnight while leading.

The Rondeau/Jaussaud Group 6 entry had failed to qualify on the Wednesday due to metering unit and (two) ignition box breakages. On Thursday the car refused to run: yet another ignition box was changed. The problem was eventually traced to one rogue wire - just in the nick of time to make the race. At the weekend the only problem was a reluctant starter motor which required cold water coaxing! That caused anxiety for Rondeau and Jaussaud when each took a turn to spin out on the circuit!

But the car was kept going and shrugged off a late challenge from Ickx' Porsche 936. So it was that Rondeau and his trusty helpers were invited to share a glass of champagne with President Giscard d'Estang, celebrating the first ever Le Mans win for a driver/constructor, and the first for an inhabitant of the town.

RONDEAU
3 SERIES 1981-88
COSWORTH

Rondeau's win opened the sponsorship floodgates and for 1981 no less than five cars were entered, all in M379C configuration. The rear aerofoil had grown to fit across the full width of the tail and there were smaller windscreens on the three Group Six cars, two of which were running 3.3 litre DFL engines.

Just over two hours into the race the 3.0 litre Group Six car of Lafosse crashed on the Mulsanne straight killing the driver.

The Tambay/Pescarolo car with a Mader 3.3 DFV suffered engine problems which eventually stranded it out on the circuit with a flat battery. The Rondeau/Jaussaud car with a Cosworth-built DFL was out soon after with handling difficulties caused by a broken chassis. The surviving GTP cars of Haran/Schlesser/Streiff and Spice/Migault were second and third overall, the French trio winninig the class.

1982 found Rondeau running a full programme of races in the first year of Group C. The M382 was an interim design, the team awaiting completion of its new ground effect M482 chassis. The new car was troubled and raced just once, during the whole season; the stop gap machine then became the mainstay of the '82 works effort.

The M382 chassis was essentially that of its predecessor fitted with the inboard rear suspension and revised brakes of the ground effect car. A longer tail section with squarer aerofoil supporting fins distinguished the newcomer from the M379. Electrical problems in practice and the race caused by the notorious vibration problem inherent in 3.9 litre DFL engines affected the entire works three car Le Mans team.

Migault/Spice/Lapeyre managed to lead early on until they came to an ignition sensor failure induced halt at Arnage and Pescarolo/Ragnotti/Alliot joined them a

short while later with a similar fault. Jaussaud/Rondeau ran in the top ten during the early hours until a forty minute pit stop dropped them down the field before finally retiring with a dropped valve in the ninth hour. Haran's ex works M379C retired just short of half distance with engine failure. Bussi's M382 managed a fifteenth place finish despite a troublesome clutch while Yver with another ex-works M379C finished tenth and added to the so-nearly triumphant Rondeau score for the Manufacturers' title.

Porsche ruled in '83 with works and customer cars. However three M382s and an M379C were entered at Le Mans. A 3.3 litre M381 and the 3.0 M379C were factory entries backing up the still unimpressive M482. The 3.3 car of Lapeyre/Snobeck/Cudini was only a couple of seconds slower than the M482s in practice but was retired after two hours, a water leak having caused the engine to overheat. The 379C driven by Elford/Verney/Gouhier ran reliably into the top twenty but the engine broke after ten hours. The two surviving 382s finished 19th and 20th, Guuitteny/De Dryver/Yver in the latter's car leading home Herregods/Witmeur/Libert in Bussi's example.

1984 saw the Bussi and Yver machines running again with a 379C owned by Grand competing in the C2 category. The C2 car was the only survivor, finishing eleventh overall and second in class.

In 1985 Bussi's car was driven to 15th place by Justice/Sotty/Oudet while Yver's car retired just after midnight with a broken engine. For the 1986 race Patrick Oudet shared his M382 with Justice until the oil pressure faded while the M379C of Del Bello/Sotty and new owner Roussiaud, running in C2, finished 17th. Bussi's car was entered for the 1987 race but failed to appear. However, the following year a 379C (actually the third placed car in 1980) finished but was unclassified.

RONDEAU
4 SERIES
COSWORTH

The Rondeau M482 was intended to be the car with which Jean Rondeau would mount a serious challenge for the World Endurance Championship in 1982. Given the impressive track record of the preceding 3 Series cars the new design was eagerly awaited. It had an aluminium monocoque designed and produced in house and rocker arm rear suspension. A 3.95 litre DFL engine was mounted as a fully stressed member once it was available, coupled to a Hewland gearbox.

The car featured futuristic bodywork designed by Max Sardou of March and Lola T600 fame. It had a chisel shaped nose, side mounted radiators and sweeping rear end treatment above the largest venturi tunnels yet seen on a prototype racing car. A relatively narrow rear wing was mounted on fins which extended up from the exagerated diffuser side panels. Delays led to the car making its debut at Silverstone in 1982 where it retired with serious overheating. The team resolved to rely on 3-series machines for the rest of the season.

Extensive winter testing saw cooling improved, the nose now carrying a water radiator while a wider aerofoil was fitted at the rear. The revised car was intended to

run the turbocharged DFL but Ford axed that project. Thus, Rondeau arrived at Le Mans 1983 with regular DFLs. The aerodynamics proved over-efficient in terms of downforce, slowing the cars and causing alarming 'porpoising' on the Mulsanne. The three entries retired with engine problems.

Towards the end of 1983 the Rondeau company went into receivership but a low key one car entry was made for the 1984 Le Mans race. A 482 with revised underbody, it finished 14th. By 1985 all the cars racing were in the hands of privateers and the two that appeared at Le Mans both retired before half distance. The following year a single entry from Graff Racing finished the race 13th. The same car finished one place higher in 1987.

RONDEAU	COSWORTH
4 series - 1982	90 degree V8
Alloy monocoque	3.9 litres
Suspension:	Alloy block
wishone front	Fuel injected
rocker arm rear	32 valves
Engine stressed	d.o.h.c.
Hewland gearbox	Unblown
Ground effect car	550b.h.p.

LOLA T600 COSWORTH

Eric Broadley's T600 design was the car that introduced ground effect technology to Le Mans. The chassis was a full length aluminium honeycomb monocoque with an integral roll cage, wishbone suspension having inboard coil spring/dampers and hub mounted ventilated disc brakes. Anti roll bar settings and brake balance were adjustable from the cockpit and the car ran on 16 inch BBS rims. A compressed-air operated jacking system was fitted and fuel was carried in two flank mounted, rubber lined cells. Provision was made for the chassis to accept a wide range of engines in Group 6 and IMSA use.

The bodywork was of glassfibre reinforced plastic with Nomex protection in heat sensitive areas. Initial aerodynamic designs were carried out by Max Sardou of the French S.E.R.A. company although changes were made by Lola design staff during subsequent wind tunnel tests. A full length ground effect underbody was activated by air passing under a nose splitter into venturi tunnels with steeply angled diffusers running through the rear suspension (which were, however, kept as clear as possible of obstructions).

Water radiators were side mounted and were ventilated by large NACA type ducts on each flank. Oil cooling was by heat exchanger. The doors hinged forward on either side of a wrap around wind screen, the cockpit roof tapering toward the rear of the car allowing a clean airflow onto the rear wing which was mounted on twin vertical fins with additional gearbox-anchored central supports.

A Group 6 version of the car, fitted with a 3.3 litre Cosworth DFL engine and a Hewland DG gearbox was run in a full 1981 season programme by GRID racing, a company formed by Guiseppe Risi and Ian Dawson. The car was driven by Briton, Guy Edwards and Spaniard, Emilio de Villota Edwards legendary sponsor bagging abilities ensuring that it was well backed by a multitude of companies.

At Le Mans a second Spaniard, Fernandez, was seconded to the drivinig strength. Unfortunately, at the Sarthe circuit the design's main strength, its underbody-generated effect, worked against speed on the long straight and the drivers could manage no better than 11th fastest in practice. More worryingly, the engine had begun to show the signs of a vibration problem that would seriously affect many future DFL engine users.

After a race fraught with problems including a spin, an oil leak, a split oil cooler and clutch and gearbox gremlins the car was classified 16th 67 laps behind the winner. A second T600 chassis had been entered by the American Cooke-Woods Racing this car fitted with a twin turbo 3.2 litre Porsche 935-type flat 6 engine reputed to produce 820 bhp. Fancied by some as an outsider for victory, the car encountered early problems caused by the neccesity of mounting the wide engine high in the chassis to avoid fouling the air tunnels which played havoc with the rear suspension geometry. A solution was found, only for the team to discover than an experimental exhaust system was adversley affecting turbo boost pressure, reducing engine power to 300 bhp. In desperation it removed the ground effect underbody in the hope of increasing straight line speed but despite the efforts of star drivers Redman and Rahal the car failed to qualify.

LOLA	COSWORTH
T600 - 1981	90 degree V8
Honeycomb monocoque	3.3 litres
Suspension:	Alloy block
wishbone front	Fuel injected
wishbone rear	32 valves
Engine stressed	d.o.h.c.
Hewland gearbox	Unblown
Ground effect car	520b.h.p.

A GO AT LE MANS

Lola built one of the first of the new generation Group C/GTP Sports-Prototypes, initially for IMSA GTP racing in 1981. However, the T600 model could be run at Le Mans in that transitional year as a Group 6 car and Brian Redman and Guy Edwards could not resist the challenge. Allan Staniforth asked them about their projects.

The arrival of Ground Effect at Le Mans was not only somewhat low key, but also a little late considering the transformation that aerodynamic downforce had wrought in Formula One.

It came about as much from a casual remark by long-distance racer Brian Redman as from any careful pre-planning. He made it to Eric Broadley at Lola, one of the more fertile and wide ranging minds in racing car design, who had during 1980 already completed the design of a full venturi-tunnelled IMSA GTP Prototype to take a wide variety of engines, the T600.

Redman was driving for the American Cooke-Woods team which was planning to buy two T600s to race in IMSA's new GTP category with Porsche and Chevrolet power units, and while visiting the Lola factory he suggested "a go at Le Mans". But implementing it would require money, drivers, organisation, and backing. It was a situation tailor-made for Guy Edwards, perhaps the most successful sponsorship finder motor racing has seen, as well as a notably courageous and capable driver himself.

Hearing of the existance of the new design he took it up with Eric Broadley, proposing a "works entry" - Lola to supply a loan car, while he would find the engine, drivers, cash and organisational back up. At the same time the American team would field an 800 bhp Porsche twin turbo Le Mans car for Redman and US driver Bobby Rahal after installing the engine in California.

It is ironic that Redman and his partner were destined to get nowhere in the race after huge engine installation and intercooler problems made the car so late it was still having its paint job finished in its Le Mans garage by a local painter three days before the flag fell.

By contrast, and adopting barely half the power from a 3.3 litre DFL but with the balancing virtues of a known quantity with few problems to get it into the car, the Edwards venture was up and testing by April. It meant the car could have two serious races under its belt before it went to La Sarthe - the Monza and Silverstone 1000 km events. And it proved to be immediately on the pace, at least for anywhere that did not have the Mulsanne straight.

Nearly a decade later, Edwards can still laugh at the furore the T600 caused with the Italian scrutineers. "We had enormous difficulties because they didn't know what they were looking at - but it got through in the end".

To be fair, what they were having to check out was a state of the art Group C car with honeycomb construction and a full aerodynamic downforce package they were unlikely to have seen before. Its specification was a very full one, with many aspects not seen or required in single seater racing, including the hidden robustness of parts and materials essential to keep a car reliable and running for 24 rather than two hours.

Chassis - a full length monocoque ran through from the brake master cylinders to a transverse plate bulkhead behind the engine. Single alloy sheet and honeycomb were combined with steel loadbearing members at critical points such as the top mountings for the front coil spring/damper units, all joints being glued and rivetted. The side pontoons did double duty as stressed sections of the tub while having contoured undersides forming part of the venturi air tunnels on each side of the car.

Bodywork - five main sections in both fibreglass and Nomex honeycomb mouldings. The doors hinged forward and, together with the roof and windscreen could be removed entirely in the case of the need to replace a broken screen. Spats covered the rear wheels, and considerable wind tunnel testing had produced the basic shape together with an adjustable front splitter, rear stabliser fins and rear wing. Only later was Edwards to find this beautiful configuration also either soaked or roasted a driver depending on the weather.

Suspension - Lola's own cast magnesium uprights were used both front and rear, together with coil springs surrounding Bilstein gas filled damper units mounted on the lower wishbone at the front, and on to a projecting lug at the base of the rear upright. Tubular anti roll bars with blades adjustable from the cockpit by the driver gave a considerable freedom for altering the handling with the major changes in fuel load, tyre grip or weather to be expected in long distance racing. That at the front had drop links down to the bottom wishbone while at the rear the top wishbone extended inboard to become a rocking arm with a bush at the end ot accept the ball-ended tip of a blade. The lower rear wishbone also incorporated a link threaded left/right at each end to give speedy and accurate adjustment of toe on the driving wheels.

Steering - Rack and pinion, of course, of Lola's own design and construction held in alloy mounting clamp blocks, themselves bolted to the substantial alloy plate front bulkhead. The column was adjustable for both height and reach, and carried an 11.5 inch black leather rimmed steering wheel. The wheel from the Le Mans car still hangs on Edwards' office wall - the only one he has ever kept as a momento from a long and successful career.

Driver safety - In many ways the Lola was well ahead of its time in looking possible disaster fully in the face, not least in having the driver's footwell area both double skinned and rigid foam filled. The cockpit roll cage was double hooped, one in the normal position behind the driver and another running across the top of the windscreen aperture, the mountings being given triangulation plates into the tub to spread the loads into the honeycomb sides. Honeycomb sides and rear bulkheads provided barriers against flame or fuel while the rubberised fuel cells were also protected by outer walls of "crushable structure" - honeycomb and rigid foam. A six-point quick release harness held the driver in place, but still with freedom to reach the buttons for electronically operated fire extinguisher system and life support air bottle.

Engine installation - With not totally dissimilar dimensions, both the Chevrolet and Cosworth V8s formed the basis of fittings in the engine bay, which included a magnesium gearbox adapter plate, engine mountings and suggested exhaust systems. Lola's literature mentioned "other options to be arranged" but there proved to be many difficulties for the car 6000 miles away having a Porsche flat six installed.

Cooling - The buyer theoretically had little more to do than run some rubber, alloy or Aeroquip piping from his engine to the installed swirl pot and header tank. Twin radiators and a heat exchanger for oil were already installed in the side pontoons, together with the necessary ducting and airflow arrangements, courtesy earlier wind tunnel testing.

Fuel system - Fuel was not centrally mounted as in Formula One but was held in flexible rubber safety cells, one on either side of the car. Pumps took the fuel to a combined collector pot and filter with one way valves guarding against surge and momentary starvation. Once again, the new owner had barely more than a length of aeroquip to install to be in business. Aircraft type dry-break filler couplings were recessed into the body.

Lubrication system - Alloy tank for a dry sump system, complete with the necessary Aeroquip pipes and fittings.

Transmission - Dependant upon the type and power of engine to be fitted, Hewland DG and VG five speed/reverse gearboxes could be supplied, both with their own oil pump and w cooler matrix. Drive shafts carried universal joints on the inboard end with constant velocity-type at the hubs,

themselves "live" in taper roller bearings within the uprights.

Brakes - these were all outboard, with 12.5 inch ventilated discs gripped by double four pot Lockheed calipers on each wheel - a massive installation but no more than would be required to pull almost a ton of car down from - hopefully - 220 mph wherever there was space to reach such a speed. Front body ducting and internally cast ducts within the rear uprights would deal with cooling and there were normal dual systems to operate the calipers with Lockheed hydraulic master cylinders connected by a balance bar which the driver could adjust by remote cable to alter his front/rear ratio as he might prefer or need.

Wheels - Cast magnesium alloy, to take 26 inch diameter tyres on 10 or 11 inch wide front rims, and 14 or 15 inch rears. All were located on six toughened steel pegs in each hub flange with centre locknut and safety pin.

Electrical system - A lightweight 12 volt battery was kept charged by an engine driven alternator. It had a considerable task with twin fuel pumps, quadruple headlamps, twin stop/tail lights, a massive windscreen wiper motor for the single parallelogram arm needed to keep the steeply raked screen clear of water, demisting fan, washer motor and instrument lighting. Linking everything was a complex wiring harness that had to be protected from vibration, heat, chafing, water and connector trouble if the car was not to be put out by some minor insurmountable fault during a race.

Instruments - Basic but complete, providing the driver with RPM, oil pressure and temperature, water temperature and fuel pressure. Non-reflective positions and a brightness adjuster for illumination were also part of the night driving provisions.

Corrosion protection - All the suspension links as well as steel structures built into the tub were chemi-backed, anodised or kephos-finished. These methods were not only to keep rust at bay, but also permit crack-testing and checking without the risks that plating - particularly chromium - cause by putting a separate skin onto a component. All the rod ends and spherical bearings also had either their own chemical protection or were manufactured from stainless steel to begin with.

Long distance features - Endurance racing has its own difficulties and all is not necessarily lost by an unplanned pit stop. To help in such situations, the T600 had built in pneumatic jacks, two at the front and one at the rear giving virtually instantaneous jacking. The windscreen was designed for rapid removal and replacement complete with its own mounting panel. The seat harness had high speed adjustment to look after varying sizes of driver, and there was a fuel reserve linked into a warning light.

Dimensions - The wheelbase measured 106.5 inches while the front track was 62.0 inches, the rear 61.0 inches. The overall length was 186.5 inches, while the height was 41.5 inches, the width 78.5 inches and the gross frontal area was 22.6 square feet.

The racing plans and the car details were unveiled on March 27 1981, just 11 weeks before Le Mans - and six years since the factory had last shown a long distance racer.

Broadley had used the consultant services of French aerodynamicist Max Sardou during the design and production of the first shape and followed this up with a further programme with his own team at Imperial College's wind tunnel in London, making further modifications in the light of Lola's own results. The Lola team was into a new area of unskirted tunnels and very high speeds and, despite its work the Le Mans car was to fall sadly short of the hoped for top speeds of well over 210 mph.

It was planned that parallel testing and development would go on in America where Brian Redman was to lead the Cooke-Woods two car effort giving the factory further feedback. The Chevrolet engined T600 was complete and running on US road tracks by late spring, and comments from Redman's letter to the factory at that time (quoted here with his permission) give a fascinating glimpse of both good and bad points once the car was actually racing.

Included in his observations were:

"...truely excellent in all major areas - no problem areas in the structural strength."

"...one of the main problems at the moment is the fuel system. Needs better reserve, faster filling and the car quickly stops from lack of pressure if not running hard".(Edwards was later to stop irrecoverably at Silverstone when levels in the tanks fell below a certain point).

"...fuel gauge is a waste of time - we have replaced it!"

"...heavier sway (anti roll) bars needed with more effective adjusters in cockpit."

"...adjustable clutch footrest needed; mirrors moved from body to front wings; brake discs cross drilled for better feel; wire mesh stoneguards fitted ahead of radiators; louvred panels inserted in roof to aid air extraction for driver comfort."

Redman also asked for better quality electrical switches, alloy covers for the headlights, and warned of the need to frequently check rear wheelnut tightness at 150 ft/lbs torque.

In England, Edwards was completing his plans for Le Mans. He remembers it with great clarity. "I lived that car. I was with it from the beginning. I watched it being built and it was a great team effort, everyone really helping everyone else. We got the whole deal set up and running in three months. I organised Cosworth factory engines, and a great friend with whom I'd

driven many times, Emilio de Villota joined me with Ian Dawson running the team".

A third driver, Juan Fernandez, later joined the team. It was no handicap in his search for sponsorship that Edwards persuaded the BBC to send a camera team for a Tuesday Documentary on his Le Mans effort (an interesting contrast to the BBC's disinterest seven years later in Jaguar's triumph).

Edwards can now reveal that the Le Mans car was strictly speaking the second car built but was plated as number three as the US order insisted on the first two. It first raced at the Monza 1000 km, qualifying fifth but breaking a vital bolt in the rear suspension at 64 laps beyond hope of immediate repair.

The British debut at Silverstone showed huge promise. The car was second on a grid that formed up in pouring rain, went off like a rocket, had a lead of 19 seconds within the first few laps and was holding a firm first place by half distance. "It leaked

like a sieve and we were all soaked driving it, but it was superb", recalls Edwards, "then on the 94th lap coming around Stowe it died. It wouldn't pick up the last two gallons, and that was it. I walked back in the rain. Very disappointing".

The car received number 18 for Le Mans and was carrying the names of three major sponsors - Banco Occidentale, Rizla and Ultramar - as well as half a dozen smaller helpers. But all the planning had not prepared anybody for the 30 mph shortfall on the Mulsanne straight. A calculated 500 bhp with a drag co-efficient of 0.34 should have provided at least 210 mph (against Porsche promising to be over 220 mph).

"In fact we got 195 mph in qualifying and 185 mph in the race", Edwards reflects, "It dropped us 20 seconds a lap straight away and we qualified 12th at three minutes 42 seconds against Porsche on pole at three minutes 29 seconds. It was one of the hottest weekends of the year and we decided Emilio would take the start and I

would finish. As it turned out we did finish - in 16th place and still going".

Clearly, that finish was not achieved without trouble, primarily broken exhausts, oil pipes an oil seal and splitting oil cooling radiators. Edwards remembers: "the scariest part was around one am. going down the Mulsanne weaving four feet either way. I don't think anyone goes down that straight comfortably. I decided to keep it going for two more laps so that I would not come in early but it is seared on my memory. It turned out an oil cooler had split and it poured out onto one rear tyre, but we repaired it and got going again.

"There was a great deal of vibration from the DFL engine, and at four am. we had another serious oil leak".

This one turned out to be a faulty fitting "O' ring in the scavenge system which took almost an hour to rectify, and there was further delay when the car went off on oil at the Esses and needed major bodywork taping before it could re-enter the fray.

Despite the stops, the T600 crept slowly and steadily up the running order. Its position throughout 24 hours read: 51st - 46 - 39 - 33 - 23 - 23 - 31 - 32 - 33 - 31 - 30 - 29 - 26 - 26 - 26 - 25 - 24 - 23 - 21 - 20 - 17 - 16 - 16 - 16, there to finish having covered 287 laps.

By the standards of Porsche, or later on Jaguar, it had been a shoe string entry, though it had needed around £250,000 in addition to the equipment. But it was a pioneer effort. the fruits of which were to come later, notably in the race-leading T610 of the following year.

As Eric Broadley had observed to a chafing Edwards when early snags arose: "Nothing worthwhile ever happens in five minutes, Guy".

LOLA T610 COSWORTH

For the first season under Group C rules a new Lola, the T610, appeared, having a similar aluminium honeycomb monocoque although with the now mandatory single, centrally-located fuel cell. A ground effect underbody was again incorporated. On the rear suspension the coil spring/damper units were fitted high up to give clearance for the venturi tunnels.

Radiators were again side mounted but fed through door ducts on the T610, venting through outlets on the upper body ahead of the rear wheels. Initially the rear wheels were faired in but they were later left open to improve cooling of the hub mounted disc brakes. The body work on the original car featured a very short nose which carried an adjustable aerofoil mounted between twin front booms. The tail was long and slab sided with a low mounted rear aerofoil. The air tunnels beneath the car were shallow, the intention being to reduce drag. The short nose and central fuel location made for a very forward driving position which was apparently disconcerting when driving the car for the first time.

By the time of its race debut the T610 had been modified with a longer, high downforce, nose and shorter tail (Group C rules specifying a maximum overall length). The changes improved the top speed but ruined the airflow to the radiators, causing overheating. By Le Mans the cooling problems had been solved and another new nose was in place, with a flat panel replacing the nose wing. Revised brake ducts provided better cooling and headlamps mounted on ugly blisters atop the nose were also introduced.

Two cars were entered for the 1982 Le Mans race; the works Ultramar sponsored car for Edwards/Keegan and a Cooke Racing BP car for Redman/Adams, which was still using a nose wing. The works car was very fast on the straight in practice, second fastest overall behind one of the factory Porsches at 218.7mph. Its low drag ground effect was obviously working well; too well as later the undertray was sucked

off the bottom of the car.

In the race Edwards ran behind the leading Porsches in third place during the opening laps. Alas, starter motor trouble and an aerodynamic problem with the doors "belling" at high speed dropped the car back a long way. The car was running in 21st place after five hours when a head gasket blew. The American T610 had been in difficulties right at the start being pushed off the grid when fuel pump failure stalled the car. After resuscitation the car was driven forcefully by Redman, back up to 16th place at the end of the second hour. However, the effort came to nought when, due to a miscalculation, the car was stranded out of fuel on the circuit leaving the driver with a long walk back to the pits.

Plans were made for an improved version of the T610 to be run by the works in 1983 and work seemed to be progressing well until the cancellation of the factory Ford C100 project ended the development of the turbocharged DFL engine. The Lola project had been based around the new engine and was consequently abandoned.

The Cooke Racing car appeared again at the 1983 Le Mans race, fitted with the 1982 works type nose and it ran reliably, nudging into the top ten until suspension failure dropped Kent-Cooke/Adams/Servanin back before overheat sidelined them for good. The same car returned in 1984, having passed into the hands of John Bartlett. Fitted with a 3.3 litre DFL and driven by Migault/Kempton/Servanin it retired in the sixth hour when the engine broke.

LOLA	COSWORTH
T610 - 1982	90 degree V8
Honeycomb monocoque	3.9 litres
Suspension:	Alloy block
wishbone front	Fuel injected
wishbone rear	32 valves
Engine stressed	d.o.h.c.
Hewland gearbox	Unblown
Ground effect car	550b.h.p.

COSWORTH
GROUP C 'SPECIALS'

For the first running of Le Mans under Group C regulations there were no fewer than 17 entries running the Cosworth V8 engine as propulsion for a Group C 'Special'. Unfortunately, for the teams running the V8 in its enlarged guises there was a headache of increased vibration and this caused problems for almost all the special builders, giving rise to anything from loosened ancillaries to structural damage

Two enlarged versions of the DFV were available: the 3.3 and the 3.95 litre DFLs, the larger version causing the greatest vibration problem. Most seriously affected was the Sauber SHS C6, an aluminium and honeycomb monocoque car produced by Peter Sauber with a striking carbon fibre/Kevlar body by Seger and Hoffman. The C6 incorporated a nose located, top vented radiator, a ground effect underbody and a central pillar delta shaped rear wing.

Two examples were entered for Le Mans, one run by Gerhard Schneider's GS Tuning company, the other by the Swiss driver/entrant Walter Brun. The GS Tuning car had the engine carried in its own subframe to combat the vibration: to no avail since by the sixth hour the engine mountings had broken, putting the car out of the race. The Brun car suffered three vibration induced starter motor failures and was retired. In 1983 after a behind-the-scenes shuffle of personnel a replica appeared at Le Mans as a Sehcar rather than a Sauber. Driven by a trio of Canadians, it retired during the night with a broken exhaust system.

The Dome RC82's ancestry could be traced back to the two bizarre looking Cosworth cars that had run at Le Mans in '79, albeit failing to finish. The Masao Ono design was gradually refined over the ensuing seasons. A full cockpit enclosure made the car eligible for Group C in 1982 and one example was run at Le Mans by John MacDonald's March Grand Prix team.

The RC82's narrow track and aerodynamic flat bottomed shape made it fast down the Mulsanne but it was damaged in

the race morning warm up and had to pit after a token lap at the start to continue repairs, losing more than two hours. After eight hours it was retired due to a broken mount. It returned in 1983, now owned by Nick Mason and tended by Colin Bennett Racing, only to retire after eight hours with a broken gearbox. In 1984, run by the DRA it lasted 14 hours while a works entered 'RC83' had been destroyed in a massive accident in the Esses during qualifying.

The Grid S1 was an aluminium honeycomb monocoque design by Geoff Aldridge, produced and run by Ian Dawson's team, which had run the works Lola in 1981. The distinctive looking car was styled so as to promote air flow to its underwing. In 1982 it was qualified a hopeful 17th at Le Mans running a 3.3 litre DFL but was the first retirement with a broken piston after 39 minutes. In 1983 it ran a 3.95 litre DFL which broke after seven hours.

Yves Courage competed regularly at Le Mans in the late Seventies and in 1982 became a constructor in his own right with the Cougar C01 Le Mans special. This was a flat bottom, high sided monocoque chassis to his own design propelled by a 3.3 litre DFL. Suspension was conventional and cooling was by twin side mounted radiators. The g.r.p. body was designed by ex-Renault aerodynamicist Marcel Hubert and featured gull wing doors and a high mounted rear aerofoil.

In the 1982 race the CO1 retired after 10 hours with a broken gearbox while in 1983 a revised CO1B proved very quick on the Mulsanne but retired when the engine failed. In 1984 an improved CO2 boasting suspension and aerodynamic revisions was the quickest Cosworth qualifier but suffered an oil pump failure after 13 hours.

The de Cadenet was a low budget project based on an old Lola Group 6 chassis with a DFV and bulbous bodywork. The car was built and run by ADA Engineering and retired from the 1982 race when it ran out of fuel before the five hour mark.

FORD C100 COSWORTH

The Ford C100 prototype was born in 1981 prior to the confirmation of Group C regulations. It was based around a Len Bailey designed aluminium monocoque and outwardly was distinguished by a smooth upper body surface and a very forward driving position, accentuated by a long tail which terminated in a low mounted full width aerofoil. A full ground effect underbody was incorporated in the design with cooling by side mounted radiators which expended air through ducts on the underside of the car. However, soon the ground effect underbody was abandoned and a more conventional cooling system was fitted.

The definitive Group C C100 was built over the winter of 81/82, based around the Bailey design with alterations by Eberhard Braun. Its body shape followed extensive wind tunnel tests and had large ducts cut into the flanks for side mounted water radiators and a nose mounted oil radiator. The design again incorporated ground effect and the rear aerofoil was mounted on a central structure atop the gearbox.

Early in the 1982 season the project was taken over by the Zakspeed team which produced a heavily revised machine devised by Tony Southgate. The tub remained, as did a DFL engine and a Hewland gearbox but these were no longer mounted on a tilt. The rear suspension was new and the oil radiators were repositioned in the flanks while there was a new g.r.p. body with a wide smooth nose and a low mounted rear aerofoil. Two examples were entered for Le Mans, equipped with 3.95 litre DFL engines. Both were over 60 kg overweight and neither could get much over 200 mph on the Mulsanne.

Having qualified sixth and 11th, the C100s ran in the leading group early in the race, Winkelhock actually leading at the four hour mark. Soon his car was hit by clutch problems then engine failure sidelined it. The other car stopped out on the circuit with a vibration induced electrical failure.

Southgate designed a new C100 to be raced with a turbo engine in 1983 only for Ford to axe the project. An ex-Zakspeed C100 appeared at Le Mans in 1983 run by the Peer Racing team only to run out of fuel on the Mulsanne after 16 laps.

FORD	COSWORTH
C100 - 1982	90 degree V8
Alloy monocoque	3.9 litres
Suspension:	Alloy block
wishbone front	Fuel injected
wishbone rear	32 valves
Engine semi-stressed	d.o.h.c.
Hewland gearbox	Unblown
Ground effect car	550b.h.p.

POINTLESS EXERCISE

The coming of Group C inspired the return of Ford as an entrant of endurance cars. The Ford C100 was the Eighties answer to the legendary GT40. It arrived in 1981 and left in 1983 with one full season under its belt. A season in which Ford scored not a single World Endurance Championship for Makes point.

With the impending arrival of Group C, Ford of Britain contracted Cosworth Engineering to develop a larger capacity version of its classic 3.0 litre DFV engine. Although designed as a Formula One engine, the DFV had been used in Group 6 throughout the Seventies, and of course won Le Mans in 1980 through the efforts of Rondeau. The contractual sum was £100,000 and was to be supplemented by Ford allowing Cosworth full access to its extensive technical facilities. Cosworth was first to develop a 3.3 litre big bore engine, then was to lengthen the stroke to achieve 3.9 litres.

The DFL engine was to carry the Ford blue oval on its cam covers for a period of three years and was to be made available to a team nominated by Ford, in addition to which Cosworth was free to sell and service customer engines. As 1981 progressed a number of aspiring Group C teams ordered DFL engines and Ford set up its own works Group C effort. The Group C regulations were finalized late in the day and it was immediately apparent that the DFL wouldn't produce sufficient power to be competitive in the long term, even in 3.9 litre guise. However, there was insufficient time to consider turbocharging the engine for 1982.

Meanwhile, the Ford works team had been formed through a take-over of a project by endurance racing entrant Alain de Cadenet and designer Len Bailey to produce a ground effects Cosworth car, initially for Group 6 but capable of subsequent conversion to Group C specification.

Initially it was envisaged that the car would be run from England but during its genesis it was moved to Ford's Cologne competition department. The car featured a Hesketh-manufactured aluminium tub and ran its Cosworth engine fully stressed. Since it was 100mm. high it was dubbed the C100.

The Ford C100 made its debut at Brands Hatch in 1981, inviting comparisons with the Alan Mann Ford Prototype project of 1968, which had unsuccessfully tried to build on the success of the GT40 and its derivatives. The 3.0 litre DFV powered Ford Prototype (which never made it to Le Mans) had also been designed by Bailey.

Although Ford's new Prototype had completed only 400 miles of frequently interrupted testing, it performed faultlessly at Brands securing pole position. The car was neat and tidy and obviously generated a lot of grip but in the race retired two laps after its first fuel stop due to gearbox failure.

After this promising maiden outing Ford might have seen itself on the verge of repeating the Sixties successes in sports-prototype racing. Then, the GT40 had won Le Mans four years in a row in various guises.

At the end of '81 Bailey withdrew from the project and Eberhardt Braun's revised, 3.3 litre DFL propelled, Group C legal C100 first travelled from its Ford Cologne base to Paul Ricard in February 1982 where ATS Grand Prix driver Manfred Winkelhock and Zakspeed contractee Klaus Ludwig gave the car its preliminary shake down. Only weeks before Lancia's Group 6 car had lapped the short circuit in 1m. 09s, but the best that the Ford could achieve was a disappointing 1m 13s. Compounding the embarrassment, the world's motoring press, invited along, captured for posterity pictures of the C100 lifting its inside front wheel as it rounded the French circuit's tighter turns.

After the first day's running the car had undergone extensive suspension changes. While retaining the same geometry as the car which had run at Brands Hatch, experiments were conducted with springs of varying rates, shock absorbers and anti-roll bars, the situation aggrevated by the Schmid thelm spring maker's delay in supplying the desired parts.

The C100's WEC debut had been posted as the Brands Hatch race on March 14, first round of the new series, but the Ricard problems forced Ford to withdraw the entry. Instead, it announced that the revised car would run competitively for the first time at Zolder, Belgium on March 21 in the Deutsche Rennsport Meisterschaft opener. "The results of that first test required Ford to rethink completely the C100's suspension geometry and spring rates", commented Peter Ashcroft, Director of Ford Motorsport (Europe), "the car has more downforce than we anticipated and our estimate of the spring rates required was very wrong".

Unfortunately, Zolder hardly transpired to be the upturn in fortunes Ford had envisaged and the 3.3 litre C100 (the 3.9 litre engine not yet ready) was even humbled by its Zakspeed 1.7 litre four cylinder turbo engined Capri stablemate. Ludwig qualified his Jagermeister liveried C100 fourth fastest after problems balancing the brakes and selecting fourth gear. The revised suspension, however, did improve the handling enabling Ludwig to run fourth in the race behind Klaus Neidzweidz' turbo Capri and the Porsche 935s of Bob Wollek and Rolf Stommelen. Then the C100 tangled with the latter damaging its suspension, putting Ludwig out of the race.

Another DRM round followed then the C100 made its WEC debut at Monza in April. The new chassis readied for the event arrived late for practice and only participated in the second day's timed session. Ford was criticised by the racing press for shabby preparation. The car's performance was hardly any better, with the 3.3 litre engine down on power and the chassis giving its drivers an exciting ride through Monza's fast corners. In the race, however, the C100 ran as high as third before a ruptured water pipe cooked its Cosworth engine.

Frustrated and probably under pressure from sponsors, Ford revealed soon after Monza that it had withdrawn the Jagermeister C100 from the DRM. Disappointed with its form, Ford decided to take the C100 away from the critical gaze of the German press and announced that it would not reappear in the DRM until the Norisring "Money Race" on June 27. Ford also moved preparation away from the Cologne factory to Erich Zakowski's Zakspeed premises at Neiderzissen. Having moved there, it was mooted that the DRM car would be fitted with the 1.7 litre turbo engine from the Capri: that at least would allow it blistering performance if only for a short while with the turbo boost wound up high!

Unfortunately a 1.7 litre turbocharged C100 didn't appear but for the next round of the WEC at Silverstore a completely new C100 was rolled out. A replica of the prototype had been taking shape in Britain based around an aluminium honeycomb monocoque produced by John Thompson. This had been intended for de Cadenet to race but in the light of the problems with the prototype it had been adopted by Ford as the basis of a second-generation C100.

The model had been revamped from stem to stern, saving 70kg. in weight and retaining only the uprights from the original design. Tony Southgate, former BRM, Shadow and Lotus Formula One designer, was responsible for the revisions, which had kept Zakspeed so busy that it had not been able to find time to build a second example. However, Ford pointed out that there was no point in producing a replica until the specification had been finalized so only one car was entered.

This time Ford appeared to have got it right. For the first time ever a C100 had managed to lap the Nurburgring short circuit, on race rubber, faster than a Group Five Capri's best on qualifiers. Winkelhock qualified the honeycomb chassis car fourth fastest for the Silverstone race and he and Ludwig had it in third place before the seemingly inevitable problems set in. A blocked fuel filter had disrupted practice but it was a fuel pump, on the lefthand tank, which gave trouble in the race. Already delayed by a puncture, the C100 had to refuel early because the pump would not deliver the bottom 20 litres of the tank. The car pressed on but first a split radiator then a failing clutch dropped it down the field.

Disappointed but now primed with optimism, Zakspeed arrived at the Nurburgring for the ADAC 1000km expecting to do well. With the classic race very close to Le Mans many teams, including Porsche, had chosen not to participate and the C100 grabbed the opportunity to shine. The fuel pumps had been relocated and remounted on rubber in the side pods to prevent a repetition of the Silverstone problem. The nose cone was also reprofiled for greater downforce and the suspension was slightly softened. Winkelhock and Ludwig, with years of Nurburgring experience behind them, had no trouble in putting the car on pole position. It was the highlight of the C100's season.

There were more fuel pressure problems in the race, the gauge indicating there simply wasn't any above 8,000rpm, but the Southgate car took the lead from the green light and held it for four hours. Then Ludwig staggered into the pits where mechanics worked feverishly on the left-hand side of the transmission. The C100 tried to rejoin the race after makeshift repairs but the differential finally seized completely a few yards down the pit lane.

At last, a second honeycomb C100 was ready for Le Mans and, from this stage onwards, Ford ran two WEC cars, for Ludwig/Marc Surer and Winkelhock/Neidzweidz. A third entry had been made

for Le Mans, however, as Ford had expected to field two brand new chassis in addition to the original Southgate car. However, Zakspeed now had the promised 3.9 litre DFL engine which pushed power to 550b.h.p. - still well short of Porsche's plus-600b.h.p. potential (according to turbo boost), but there was the fuel consumption aspect to consider.

Although both C100s handled well, there was a distinct lack of straightline speed and, to make matters worse, Winkelhock's practice engine was suspected of being down on power. The cars qualified sixth and eleventh but success at La Sarthe was thwarted by the other weak link in Ford's chain, the new DFL.

Winkelhock was in the lead when he had to stop to rectify a clutch problem but, finally, the engine blew after six hours. By this time the Ludwig/Surer car was already stationary on the Mulsanne straight, stranded by electrical failure. Similar problems stopped Rondeau's remaining 3.9 litre DFL powered M382s. Was there a connection?....... To Cosworth's chagrin, there was!

The 3.9 litre DFL had been produced by combining the original 3.3 litre DFL's bigger bore with a longer stroke crankshaft. Further changes to the engine included revised fuel pump drive, new air intakes, new cylinder liners and the adoption of a crankshaft damper. That damper was an indication of where the 3.9 DFL's biggest problem lay - vibration. Virtually all the engine's users complained about it and in severe cases it led to chassis component failures. But for Ford and Rondeau at Le Mans it was the damper itself which was the catalyst of disaster. Heat caused the rubber bush to expand cutting the wires to the adjacent ignition pick up.

The problem was quickly pin pointed by Cosworth which used the 11 week gap between Le Mans and Spa Francorchamps to solve it. It produced new dampers which it tested extensively on the C100 and the Rondeau. Although the conditions of Le Mans could not be suitably simulated at Silverstone or the Nurburgring, there were no subsequent failures and by Spa all of Cosworth's customers had at least one engine to the new specification.

For Ford the Belgian race, final round of the WEC Manufacturers title chase, was much like its preceding four adventures. Once again a relative lack of speed down the straights was evident and this was a big problem given the nature of the sweeping Ardennes circuit and both cars suffered a variety of problems including broken exhaust primaries. On a partly damp track the Ludwig/Surer car briefly held second place running intermediates but as the track dried it slipped back to share its sister car's tale of woe. Ford bowed out of the first Group C Manufacturers title chase failing to score a

single point, the C100s finishing 18th and 23rd.

The C100 story was not over for at Brands Hatch, for the Drivers title race which had been postponed from March, Ford entered three examples, the third the DRM car. The weekend began badly with two of them bursting into flames during pre-meeting testing. Fuel had leaked from a faulty seal on the metering unit, igniting the engine bay. Fortunately the scorched cars, those of Winkelhock/Neidzweidz and newcomers Jonathan Palmer/Desire Wilson, were not badly damaged.

Having begun its career at Brands Hatch 12 months earlier, the C100 again took pole position for the Kent race, this time Surer managing the feat. To complete a grand day for Ford, Winkelhock shared the front row with his Swiss team mate.

As so often in the past, it all turned sour on race day. The Shell Oils 1000 began in a torrential downpour and the two fleet C100s made the most of the spray-free air ahead - running side by side. For four laps Winkelhock and Surer bounced off each other's bodywork as they circulated alongside each other in the rain. Finally this extraordinary exhibition ended when Surer lost control on a puddle and punted his team mate's car off into the barriers!

Surer continued while Winkelhock stepped from his wreck to find the race stopped. He was then transferred to the Surer car which eventually finished fifth after fuel mixture and suspension bothers, one place and one lap behind the Palmer/Wilson car, which but for a late puncture might have finished third.

One thing had been emphasised during the 1982 season: as expected, the DFL lacked competitive power even in full 3.9 litre guise. Run flat out, it could not use up the full 1000km fuel allowance so there was no choice but to turbocharge it. A project had already commenced evaluating single and twin IHI turbochargers with a target output of 700bhp at modest boost and there was also work to further tackle the vibration problem via the adoption of Lanchester-type shafts. Meanwhile, Southgate was employed to design a brand new chassis for the turbo engine. Early tests of new car using a normally aspirated 3.9 DFL were conducted at Paul Ricard in February with encouraging results.

The '83 car was set to be run by Gordon Spice Racing on behalf of the factory. Alas, before it could be equipped with its turbo engine Stuart Turner took over as Director of Motorsports in Europe and immediately axed both the existing Group C WEC and Group B rally projects. The C100 lived on in normally aspirated guise, but only as a privateer car at Le Mans. As a DRM car it won two of the National titles as its only claim to fame.

TIGA COSWORTH TURBO

In 1986 Tim Lee Davey entered a Tiga chassis for Le Mans powered by a turbo-charged Cosworth DFL engine, following the route plotted for the prematurely curtailed C100 project. The chassis was a conventional aluminium and honeycomb monocoque based on Tiga's 1985 C2 title winning design with pull rod front suspension, rocker arm rear and carbon fibre/Kevlar bodywork. The engine was a 3.3 litre DFL pressurised by twin Garrett turbochargers and equipped with a Bosch engine management system. It had been developed by former Cosworth engineer Graham Dale Jones at Terry Hoyle Engines.

Sadly, this was a low budget effort. The engine failed in qualifying rendering the car a non starter. The car re-appeared in 1988 with modifications including a front mounted water radiator, the nose revised along Jaguar lines, and flatter side body panels. Engine and exhaust revisions had also been made but the car was untested and met new car problems in qualifying. Sadly its race only lasted five laps then an electrical malfunction shut the engine down.

TIGA	COSWORTH
GC85 - 1985	90 degree V8
Honeycomb monocoque	3.3 litres
Suspension:	Alloy block
pull rod front	Fuel injected
rocker arm rear	32 valves
Engine stressed	d.o.h.c.
Hewland gearbox	Single turbo
Ground effect car	+ 600b.h.p.

JAGUAR XJR-5

In 1984 the XJR-5 became the first factory supported Jaguar to race at Le Mans since the glory days of the Fifties. That it was basically an American project didn't seem to bother the enthusiasts and if anything it prompted the building of the TWR cars that would eventually win the race.

The XJR-5 was powered by a 6.0 litre 60 degree V12, ancestry of which could be traced back to the mid Fifties when a replacement had been designed for the production-based straight six used in the D-Type. Although the V12 race engine never surfaced, a derivative powered a number of road cars and production car based racing projects of the Seventies. In 1982 it found its way into an IMSA GTP car designed by Lee Dykstra for Group 44, the crack American race team run by Bob Tullius.

Tullius had scored numerous successes in Jaguars in SCCA racing and had managed to convince a newly independent Jaguar of the value of the image boost it could gain through a prototype programme ultimately targeted upon Le Mans. By 1984 his XJR-5 was a well established IMSA competitor, the stock block, two valve V12 now producing around 650b.h.p. controlled by a Lucas Micos engine management system.

The engine was fitted as a fully stressed member in an aluminium sheet and honeycomb monocoque. Traditional suspension was fitted at each corner with the rear spring/damper units mounted high in deference to underbody diffusers. The visible bodywork of carbon fibre and Kevlar divided the air flow either side of the cockpit into ducts feeding side mounted radiators while a full width rear wing was mounted on a gearbox post. Conforming to IMSA rules, the car had a 120 litre fuel tank and the same size wheels front and rear.

Le Mans saw two the two entries qualified in circumspect fashion and by half distance the cars were running sixth and seventh. Tullius had actually managed to lead during the first round of refuelling stops. Shortly after the midway point one car stopped with a broken throttle cable while the other spun and hit the armco when a tyre blew. Both crept back to the pits. The cable was repairable but the crashed car had lost oil and the engine was seized. The survivor ran on until gearbox failure eliminated it just before noon.

Returning in 1985, the cars featured changes to the suspension, engine and aerodynamics and improved their times by 2.5 seconds over the 1984 standard. A reduction in the fuel allowance for the race, and the quality of the fuel itself, theoretically a burden to turbo rather than 'atmo' cars was actually a greater handicap to the Jaguar than its Porsche rivals and the cars were not on the race pace. One was eliminated just after half distance when the battery flattened having been parked while the driver carried out make shift repairs. The other dropped a valve in the last hour. The damaged cylinder was isolated and the car completed two laps to be classified 13th.

JAGUAR	
XJR-5 - 1984	60 degree V12
Honeycomb monocoque	6.0 litres
Suspension:	Alloy block
wishbone front	Fuel injected
wishbone rear	24 valves
Engine stressed	s.o.h.c.
Hewland gearbox	Unblown
Ground effect car	650b.h.p.

JAGUAR XJR-6/8/9

In September 1984 Jaguar appointed Tom Walkinshaw Racing to run a two car team on its behalf in the 1985 World Endurance Championship. TWR, which had won the European Touring Car Championship for Jaguar, produced a carbon fibre monocoque chassis designed by Tony Southgate (ex BRM, Shadow and Lotus). The front suspension set the coil spring/dampers over the driver's footwell while the rear set them at either end of a beam, outside the ground effect tunnels and actually within the wheel rims. Speedline 17" / 19" rims carried Dunlop Denloc tyres while the brakes were four pot AP items mounted outboard. The rear wheels were faired in while the body made provision for a horizontally mounted front radiator. A full width rear wing was mounted on a post supported by a March five speed gearbox.

The engine was the same V12 used in America but as Group C set no capacity limit it was taken out to 6.2 litres. The car debuted at Mosport, missing Le Mans in its first season. Its 1985 pace was encouraging and Jaguar's entries at Le Mans in 1986 were from TWR rather than Group 44. When the XJR-6 arrived at Le Mans it was revised aerodynamically and was lightened and had a modified rear suspension and fuel system. Big, 6.5 litre engines were fitted for the French classic and three cars were run.

After minor hastles in qualifying the cars ran in the leading group early on. One retired after seven hours when the fuel pump broke, another fell out five hours later with a broken driveshaft while the surviving car (Schlesser/Warwick/Cheever) moved into second place in the 15th hour only for a tyre to explode damaging the rear suspension two hours later.

In 1987 the TWR team came back with a new model, the XJR-8, actually a straightforward evolution of the XJR-6 featuring numerous detail changes. It also had a 7.0 litre engine and had been almost unbeatable in championship rounds prior to Le Mans. The Le Mans cars featured a tilted engine for a horizontal rear axle line (less strain on the c.v. joints), shallower ground effect tunnels and revised, shorter bodywork. Three examples were run and they qualified in formation behind the works Porsche turbocars. Early on engine failures decimated the Porsche team leaving only one 962 to stave off the Jaguars.

Jaguar lost one car after 11 hours when Percy crashed at the Mulsanne kink due to a tyre failure. The car was wrecked but the driver escaped injury. Five hours later another retirement: cracked cylinder head. The survivor was beset by problems on Sunday, including a hole in the gearbox casing, and managed no better than fifth.

Returning to Le Mans in 1988 having won the World Endurance Championship, TWR entered no less than five XJR-9LM cars two of which were run by its IMSA team. The 9LMs had smaller diameter wheels so the engine did not need to be tilted. The short body was further refined. Porsche again boosted its way to the front of the grid and the ensuing battle was one of the closest seen for many years, the outcome in doubt to the end. Eventually the Jaguar of Lammers/Dumfries/Wallace scored an emotional victory over the surviving works Porsche while the two American run Jaguars finished fourth and 16th after delays. The two other cars retired, victims of head gasket and transmission failures.

JAGUAR	
XJR-6 - 1986	60 degree V12
Composite monocoque	6.5 litres
Suspension:	Alloy block
push rod front	Fuel injected
wishbone rear	24 valves
Engine stressed	s.o.h.c.
March gearbox	Unblown
Ground effect car	700b.h.p.

THE VITAL FACTORS

Le Mans is traditionally dominated by one marque and Porsche ruled the Group C era with a grip that in the mid Eighties looked unshakeable. Then along came Jaguar's TWR challenger and a battle for supremacy raged as never before. Ian Bamsey analyses the factors it took to produce a winning car against strong, seasoned opposition.

The first 25 years of 'Supersports' cars at Le Mans opened with Ferrari the established King and were characterised by the no-holes-barred attempt of Ford, then Porsche, then Jaguar to assert itself. These marques had 100% commitment to success backed by the resources necessary to win, but none won first time out.

Experience was the key factor that initially was missing in each case. Ford bought the experience of John Wyer who had been victorious with Aston Martin at Le Mans in the Fifties but his voice was but one of many in a multi-headed corporate effort and the collective mind had plenty of learning to do. Porsche had enjoyed bags of Le Mans success with small capacity cars but its thrust to produce an outright winner was led by keen young engineers who soon found that rushing into the production of vastly more powerful machinery was a whole new ball game.

Ford and Porsche each suffered two humbling defeats before the big budget programme paid dividends. Jaguar suffered four. Jaguar's American based Group 44 organisation suffered the first two defeats then the marque's Le Mans effort was taken over by a whole new British based Group C team: Tom Walkinshaw Racing. To its credit the TWR Group C Jaguar won third time around in time honoured tradition.

Of course, resources and experience alone don't win Le Mans. Even assuming the personnel and the equipment are capable, Lady Luck's sadistic gambling game can still spell defeat. She delights in finding new ways to sideline the most bullet-proofed, most carefully driven car in the field. The only safety is in numbers. As Doctor Ferdinand Piech, Technical Director of Porsche during the 917 era, remarked to the author: "In a battle like Le Mans, the number of warships also counted".

Piech noted that in a three car team the

chances are that one car will retire through driver error and one will retire through technical problems, leaving one car which can win if, and only if, it doesn't face serious setback. Since it entered the big league under Piech's direction Porsche has always run a minimum of three cars.

Faced with the depth of Porsche representation in the late Eighties, Jaguar felt it necessary to run five cars in 1988. It feared Porsche would push a car breaking pace, safe in the knowledge that if all the factory cars broke one of its many customer cars would be around to pick up the pieces. That is precisely what happened in 1965: a customer Ferrari was left to collect the winnings.

Of course, a multi-car entry is of no benefit if the cars are not fully attuned to the special demands of Le Mans: running three or more cars would not have helped Jaguar's cause in 1985. And frankly the Group 44 team looked unlikely to win third time around. The talk around the Jaguar encampment after the second Group 44 defeat was of lack of Group C experience. The marque had to concede that an IMSA GTP car wasn't going to defeat a Porsche Group C car.

The GTP Jaguar had been developed to run to a heavier minimum weight and to a 6.0 litre maximum displacement on unlimited and very high octane fuel. At home it raced competitively against similarly heavy Porsche prototypes confined to single turbo, two valve (fully air cooled) engines. The TWR Jaguar which took over the Le Mans programme was a very different animal.

The Group 44 GTP car used an engine which was directly descended from the team's earlier Jaguar production racers. Group 44 started its Jaguar V12 racing programme with the E-type in SCCA amateur racing then took a crack at the Trans Am series with an XJ-S. The first Group 44

E-type had rolled out with blueprinted engine with lightened flywheel and the team's own six-into-one exhaust system which released 460 bhp on standard carburation. Early on the team introduced a dry sump but not much else could be done given the regulations. The Trans Am car, however, was allowed a six Weber carburettor set up to replace the standard fuel injection with which the XJ-S was equipped and which was not considered race worthy.

The six Weber kit dramatically improved breathing and the engine offered over 530 bhp from the outset and with camshaft and porting work as permitted under Trans Am rules power rose to 570 bhp and an 8,000 rpm rev limit was achieved.

With slight modifications to the cylinder heads and ancillary equipment, this 5.3 litre carburettor engine was the starting point for the Group 44 GTP adventure in 1982. However, for 1984 a full 6.0 litre version was readied and this was equipped with a Lucas Micos engine management system. Initially the Micos low pressure injection system provided better throttle response and over time it allowed the fuel consumption to be improved and also opened up the way to intake and exhaust modifications which provided more power and torque.

With technical back up from Coventry, the 6.0 litre Group 44 engine was developed to produce around 650 bhp, its best engine offering 670 bhp: a 100 bhp improvement over the period '81 - '85 which was backed by an extra 100 lb.ft. torque thanks to the increased capacity, work on the flow characteristics of the heads and the intake and exhaust improvements allowed by the Micos system. All this on high octane racing fuel as allowed by IMSA.

IMSA fuel was as high as 114 octane. At Le Mans the organisers supply mandatory fuel in the region of 98/99 octane, as per Group C regulations. Group 44's biggest problem at Le Mans in 1985 was a persistant threat of detonation. Naturally, for the meeting the compression ratio had been reduced. Nevertheless, both cars lost their engines after refuelling during the break between Wednesday's qualifying sessions. Subsequently, the timing was backed off, to the detriment of power and fuel economy. The fuel appeared to improve during the meeting but the two car team didn't dare run its timing forward again.

TWR likewise started its Jaguar involvement in production racing but didn't go Group C with the engine from its Group A XJ-S racer. In Group A there were restrictions on inlet size and valve lift and the original exhaust manifold had to be retained although pistons, camshafts and other engine internals were free. The ultimate 5.3 litre Group A engine development by TWR engine chief Allan Scott was achieved for the 1984 season when 450 bhp/ 7,300 rpm was attained: a far cry from a competitive Group C output.

With the move into Group C Scott was able to take a clean sheet of paper to design an appropriate version of the s.o.h.c. V12 with its two directly-operated, in line, upright valves. Port and combustion chamber design was clearly restricted by the two valve layout. In particular, that meant, compared to an ideal four valve layout, that the valve area was relatively small and the plug was in a less than perfect position. But Scott knew the two valve Jaguar head well and a possible four valve design by Jaguar was rejected as adding too much weight to an engine that was already top-heavy. However, the porting of the standard Jaguar head was, Scott reckoned, superbly designed: somewhere between the best of any other two valve head and a four valve race engine. With development, he managed to obtain 100% volumetric efficiency over the maximum torque period.

The original V12 had a shallow, large diameter bowl in piston crown combustion chamber with a flat head. A later 'HE' version ran a flat top piston together with a complex combustion chamber in the head, as designed by Michael May to improve fuel economy. The Group 44 GTP engine had retained a flat head. For his Group C engine Scott was free to form his combustion chamber in the piston, in the head, or combination of both. The design he opted for, crucial to the performance of the TWR Le Mans car, understandably had to remain secret. It did not follow the Group 44 development line.

By 1988 the TWR Group C engine - equipped from the outset with a sophisticated Zytek engine management system - was running a 12:1 compression ratio, in spite of the relatively poor quality fuel. The team had started with a capacity of 6.2 litres, adopting the same 78mm. crankshaft as Group 44 but going for a slightly larger - 92mm. - bore for larger valves. At the time the GTP engine was confined to 6.0 litres by GTP regulations.

Scott's very first engine - in 1985 - produced in the region of 650 bhp on pump fuel. By 1986 the TWR chassis was lighter (down to the 850kg. Group C minimum whereas the Group 44 car had been designed to a 900kg. limit) and more fuel efficient and consequently Scott could run more power. He went out to 6.5 litres with a 94mm. bore. By 1988 he had gone to 7.0 litres with an 84mm. crankshaft, achieving more mid range torque. That cut down gear shifting and helped improve fuel efficiency. Power went as high as 745 bhp/ 7,250 rpm while maximum torque was 610 lb.ft./ 6,000 rpm.

Of course, engine performance is only part of the equation. The chassis must be right, too. Again, there was stark contrast between the equipment run by Group 44

and that of TWR. Group 44's 900kg. machine was, in fact, a little over the weight break - closer to 950 than to the 850 kg. Group C minimum. It employed an aluminium monocoque whereas TWR saved weight - and Group 44 planned to do so - through the use of an advanced composite chassis. The Group 44 Le Mans car - the XRJ-5 - was a development from a very competitive Can Am design by Lee Dykstra, with the long Jaguar block in place of the Can Am car's Chevrolet V8.

TWR XJR-6/8/9 designer Tony Southgate sat down with a clean sheet of paper and aimed for a preferred weight distribution. His 850 kg. machine set the very heavy engine further forward. In effect, Southgate sunk the front of the long block through a recess in the rear bulkhead into space that otherwise would have been occupied by part of the central fuel tank. The tank in turn extended forwards.

Compared to Dykstra, Southgate had better access to a sophisticated rolling road wind tunnel, and was able to expend more time developing an aerodynamic package specifically for Le Mans. Like so many teams, Group 44 had gone to Le Mans with a regular aerodynamic package which was then tuned as well as possible to the special demands of the circuit. That approach is at best a poor compromise.

The drawback of the standard car approach was highlighted following the arrival of the ground effect sports-prototype by teams, in extreme cases, having to revert to a flat bottom for adequate Mulsanne speed. The 1985 EMKA was just one example of that. Lift means drag and early ground effect prototypes had so much negative lift that speed on the three and threequarter mile straight proved woefully inadequate. Where negative lift - downforce - is supplied by a wing it is simple to adjust: altering the angle of attack of the wing increases or decreases lift and drag. And changing the wing itself - perhaps for a smaller version, or one with less elements - is hardly a major task. But where negative lift is supplied by a carefully shaped underbody adjustment is another matter altogether.

Le Mans is unique in the speeds attained on the Mulsanne and in the importance of drag reduction. The faster 'ordinary' Group C circuits - such as Silverstone - saw top speeds in the region of 180 mph. Le Mans added 40 mph or more to that. Now consider the fact that downforce increases as the square of speed and it will be appreciated how much it increased as high download ground effect cars got up to speed on the Mulsanne.

Reverting to a flat bottom and rear wing package was a poor compromise since an underbody produces a given amount of downforce for less drag than a wing. The ideal Le Mans car had an underbody producing just the right amount of downforce to

strike the optimum balance between speed on the Mulsanne and the requirements of the rest of the circuit, its wing acting merely as a trim tab. Striking that balance and minimising drag was the key.

Le Mans was the only circuit where drag rather than lift was the overriding consideration. TWR went to Le Mans for the first time in 1986 with a distinctly different aerodynamic package, the fruit of intensive wind tunnel testing. Externally, the car was characterised by an elongated tail and a smaller, lower set rear wing. Underneath the profile of the underbody was altered in a subtle way.

For 1987 there was another Le Mans special, further removed from the regular sprint race car's aerodynamics with an equally subtle reprofiling of the nose in addition to tail and wing and underwing modifications. It was characterised by a lack of the usual rear wheel fairings to assist the mechanics.

Interestingly, the XJR-8LM had its engine/ transaxle tilted to provide a less severe working angle for the driveshafts, in the interest of c.v. joint reliability. This had the effect of making the car more difficult to drive: although the angle of tilt was only 2.5 degrees from the horizontal plane, the drivers felt the top heavy engine was trying to come over their shoulder!. The 1988 car was designed with smaller (17" rather than 19") rear wheels which allowed a reversion to a horizontal drivetrain and reduced the height of the rear arches, assisting the quest to reduce drag. The catch was in smaller, harder worked (higher rpm) tyres - Dunlop development made the change possible.

For 1988 Southgate had produced yet another, further improved aerodynamic package, now with the spats back on. It was intended to maintain the same speed on the Mulsanne but with more downforce, notably for tackling the Porsche curves which constitute a fair proportion of the circuit. In fact, as the team ran more power, and following resurfacing of the Mulsanne, top speed actually increased. The 1988 Le Mans winning car was the product of over 400 runs over the years of 20% scale model Le Mans cars in the Imperial College rolling road wind tunnel. Although the '88 car looked to the eye as though it was a "short tail" machine, in aerodynamic terms it worked like a traditional "long tail" car. The air saw its low set wing as an extension of the tail rather than as a wing in its own right.

The fact that the team could run more power was back to experience. Quite simply, in 1987 it had underestimated how much fuel it would burn. In 1988 it got the 24 hour equation just right and it had only a few litres left in the car that finally ended the long Porsche rule at Le Mans.

LANCIA LC1 & LC2

Lancia won world titles in 1979, 1980 and 1981 but it was clear that its 1.8 litre turbo engine would not be competitive in Group C, given the generous fuel allowance. However, it was able to run its Group 6 spyder in 1982 complete with sliding skirts and weight advantage and won a number of races, though both cars run at Le Mans retired with engine related problems before half distance. For 1983 Lancia had no choice but to produce a Group C coupe and it equipped this with a Ferrari engine. At the same time the LC1 spyder was sold to the Siva Motors team which reworked the chassis to conform to Group C regulations, complete with cockpit enclosure and mandatory flat bottom area. Two examples of the underpowered machine were run at Le Mans (one by a French team) and both finished, albeit unclassified after head gasket failures.

The LC2 works car, like the LC1 was a Dallara design utilising a similar aluminium monocoque. The engine was a 2.6 litre Ferrari V8 fitted with twin KKK turbochargers and rated 620 bhp at race boost. The engine was equipped with a Marelli Weber engine management system and fed its power through a Hewland gearbox. The chassis carried an evolutionary carbon fibre/Kevlar body with nose radiator and side mounted intercoolers and ground effect underbody above which was a wide fin-mounted wing.

At Le Mans in 1983 the two works LC2s qualified second and fourth only to retire with transmission and turbocharger problems while a privately entered car went out

with a broken engine. In 1984 the LC2 returned to La Sarthe with better fuel consumption from a more powerful 3.0 litre engine and a more reliable Abarth developed gearbox. Aerodynamic changes were also evident. In the absence of the Porsche works team the works LC2s qualified first and second and both led at various stages only to hit problems. Wollek/Nannini finished eighth overcoming transmission trouble while Baldi/Barilla/Heyer suffered a broken camshaft in the 20th hour. A private entry retired before half distance with a blown head gasket.

At the 1985 Le Mans race two works cars appeared with further revisions to the bodywork and widened track allowing bigger venturi tunnels. The engine was reputedly producing 850 bhp in qualifying. Third on the grid, the Wollek/Nannini car led for the first three laps but fell back with turbo trouble. Eventually it finished sixth, just ahead of the sister car of Pescarolo/Baldi.

The Lancia Group C effort finished in 1986 but a private LC2 appeared at Le Mans in 1988 run by the Dollop team. It failed to make an impression and eventually retired with a broken transmission.

LANCIA	FERRARI
LC2 - 1983	90 degree V8
Alloy monocoque	2.65 litres
Suspension:	Alloy block
wishbone front	Fuel injected
wishbone rear	32 valves
Engine stressed	d.o.h.c.
Hewland gearbox	Twin turbo
Ground effect car	620b.h.p.

MAZDA 757 & 767

In 1983 Mazda put its twin rotor type 13B engine into a purpose-built type 717C sports-prototype chassis, most notable for its novel aerodynamic approach. A two car team was entered in the newly constituted Group C Junior (later C2) category, 12th and 18th overall and first and second in class resulting.

For 1984 Mazda representation expanded to four cars; two 727C works chassis (developments of the stubby little machines of the previous year) plus a pair of American-entered Lola T616s. All were running the 13B engine and were entered in the C2 class. By the finish Mazda engined cars held first, third, fourth and sixth in C2 with the Lola class winner tenth overall. In 1985 two 737Cs (evolved from their predecessors) were third and sixth in the C2 class, 19th and 24th overall, giving Mazda a 100% finishing record in the C2 category.

For 1986 a new triple rotor type 13J engine was developed and a two car team was entered in the IMSA GTP category. The chassis, to a design by Briton Nigel Stroud, had an aluminium honeycomb monocoque with a carbon fibre top section while the engine was carried as a semi-stressed member. Rear suspension was by rocker arms, the front was pullrod and inboard coil-spring/damper units were fitted all round. Cast iron ventilated Brembo discs were mounted on the hubs, operated by single calipers. Twin water and oil radiators were situated on the monocoque behind the line of the doors through which air was ducted to them. Hot air was vented upwards over the tail ahead of the rear wheels. The bodywork of carbon fibre with Kevlar reinforcement was distinguished by a smooth rounded nose with small splitters at either edge, the centre section being left open to induce airflow beneath the car for the ground effect underbody. A twin boom tail section was surmounted by a full width aerofoil supported on two shallow fins with an additional central strut.

The engine was formed from three 654cc rotary units which under the current equivalency formula of multiplying by 1.8 gave a displacement of 3531cc. The power output was quoted as 450bhp at 8500rpm . The transmission was a triple plate Borg and Beck clutch in a Mazda bellhousing mated to a Porsche differential and an inverted Porsche five speed gearbox.

In the race the legendary Mazda reliability was nowhere to be seen, both cars suffering terminal transmission failures. Kennedy/Galvin/Dieudonne climbed as high as thirteenth but went out after eleven hours while Yorino/Katayama/Terada retired after four hours. Technical problems led to the abandoning of a planned turbocharged engine so Mazdaspeed returned to Le Mans with two normally aspirated 757s in 1987. One chassis had lighter bodywork and a lightened engine, the other was one of the 1986 unchanged cars. Yorino/Katayama/Terada qualified 27th in the new car with Kennedy/Galvin/Dieudonne 28th, but a super-reliable run in the race by the European crew gave them a seventh place overall finish and the GTP class. The Japanese trio had been in tenth place overall at the two hour mark, but unfortunately an engine failure caused their retirement a short while later.

A single 757 appeared in 1988 providing back up for two new 767 cars which were similar apart from having four rotor engines, and also ran in GTP. Despite being five seconds slower in qualifying the older car finished ahead of its newer team mates in 15th overall driven by Terada/Kennedy/Dieudonne and again won GTP .

MAZDA	
757 - 1986	3 rotor
Honeycomb monocoque	= 3.5 litres
Suspension:	Alloy unit
pull rod front	Fuel injected
rocker arm rear	Unblown
Engine semi-stressed	450b.h.p.
Porsche gearbox	
Ground effect car	

SAUBER C8 MERCEDES

Having missed the Le Mans race in 1984 Sauber returned in 1985 with a new car powered by a mildly turbocharged Mercedes V8 engine. Fitted with two KKK turbochargers boosting at 0.7 bar the M117's power output for racing was quoted as 650 bhp at 7000rpm. The ubiquitous Hewland transmission was employed, a VG five speed in this instance. The engine was mounted in a tubular steel subframe which attached to the rear suspension, the spring/damper units of which were located on top of the bellhousing and were actuated by fabricated tubular rocker arms. The front suspension was a conventional double wishbone arrangement. Ventilated disc brakes were hub mounted with a single calipers, front/rear balance being adjustable from the cockpit. 16 inch BBS rims were fitted with Dunlop tyres. Outwardly the Sauber was similar in appearance to the same-monocoque C7 with side mounted water radiators fed by door ducts and two turbocharger intercoolers beneath fed by NACA ducts in the flanks. Side vented exhaust pipes along with the inboard rear suspension allowed clear venturi tunnels beneath the car, air entering through a cutaway beneath the concave nose panel. A lack of sufficient sponsorship meant that Le Mans would be the cars' first racing appearance with Quester/Nielsen drivinig.

On the first practice day the Sauber-Mercedes was 14th fastest but was second fastest through the Mulsanne speedtrap at 221 mph. The next day after an engine change and boost pressure problems the car flew ... literally. Coming down the straight the C8 took off at the hump between the kink and Mulsanne corner, executed a double somersault, landed back on its wheels still under power and crashed into the barriers at the side of the track. Nielsen was unhurt but the car was too badly damaged to race.

For 1986 a sponsorship deal was concluded with the Yves Saint Laurent fashion house to promote its Kouros brand which saw the C8 appear in a superb dark blue and silver livery. Winter testing continued the development of the car and by its debut at Monza the oil radiator had been relocated in the nose which now carried a splitter on its forward edge. Goodyear tyres were also new. The car ran at Silverstone prior to a two car team being entered for Le Mans.

Frustratingly, the Saubers proved slower on the straight than in 1985 and lined up 13th and 16th on the grid. Pescarolo, sharing with Danner and Quester, stopped out on the circuit within minutes of the start. The oil radiator was holed; the three time winner managed to get the car back to the pits after makeshift repairs but over an hour had been lost. Thackwell/Nielsen experienced handling difficulties before retiring with a broken engine in the seventh hour. The Pescarolo C8 got going again but lasted just two hours longer than its sister machine when the transmission failed.

A C8 returned for the 1987 Le Mans race, having been sold to the French Del Bello team. Painted in a rather garish purple with sunburst effects the car was driven by a trio of inexperienced French drivers. Unfortunately, the clutch was damaged in the race morning warm up and, despite rapid repairs, the car retired after just four laps. Undeterred, the Del Bello team entered Le Mans again in 1988 with De Dryver/Santal and Del Bello himself driving. The former qualified the car 27th and it became the sole representative of the marque when the works car were withdrawn. A reliable run got the car into the top twenty only for the engine to break during the night.

SAUBER	MERCEDES
C8 - 1985	90 degree V8
Aluminium monocoque	5.0 litres
Suspension:	Alloy block
wishbone front	Fuel injected
rocker arm rear	16 valves
Engine semi-stressed	s.o.h.c.
Hewland gearbox	Twin turbo
Ground effect car	+ 650b.h.p.

SAUBER C9 MERCEDES

Derived from the C7 and C8 Le Mans cars the 1987 Sauber-Mercedes chassis was a further refined version of the earlier models and the team enjoyed continuing support from Daimler-Benz. The C9 retained an aluminium monocoque but numerous detail changes had been made, the most notable of which was the positioning of the rear spring/damper units horizontally and longitudinally along the top engine support cradle tubes and operated through rockers. A combined water and oil radiator was mounted in the nose while air/air intercoolers for the twin KKK turbochargers were side mounted and were fed by NACA ducts. A new Kevlar sandwich body included a nose splitter and higher rear arches over BBS 19" rims. This in turn raised the rear wing mounting and gave the car a more purposeful look.

The engine had been further developed by Heini Mader and with lighter materials 12kg. had been saved while a Bosch Motronic M1.7 engine management system as fitted to the Porsche/TAG Formula One engine was employed. On its Silverstone debut the new model led in Thackwell's hands and the two examples entered for Le Mans were very much dark horses. Both qualified in the top 10 and Dumfries ran in fourth place early on and later set a lap record before retiring with gearbox failure. The other car had a torrid time visiting the catch fencing before a driveshaft coupling uncoupled. Pescarolo managed a makeshift repair and limped home only to find the team had packed up! Hurried repairs ensued but the car retired for good near midnight with another transmission failure.

For 1988 the full might of Mercedes was openly behind Sauber and the C9 design was revised and was equipped with a factory prepared engine. The team provided the only serious challenge to Jaguar's title but the eagerly awaited Le Mans confrontation with both Porsche and Jaguar was not to be. A frigtening tyre failure in the kink during qualifying prompted the team's withdrawal.

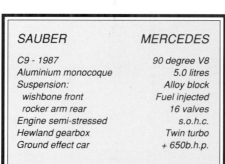

SAUBER	MERCEDES
C9 - 1987	90 degree V8
Aluminium monocoque	5.0 litres
Suspension:	Alloy block
wishbone front	Fuel injected
rocker arm rear	16 valves
Engine semi-stressed	s.o.h.c.
Hewland gearbox	Twin turbo
Ground effect car	+ 650b.h.p.

SHEER GRUNT

Daimler Benz pulled out of Le Mans after one of its cars was involved in the terrible accident of 1955. Thirty years later Peter Sauber brought the marque back, against expectations. Ian Bamsey, Editor of the International Race Engine Directory, looks at the design and development of the Mercedes V8 turbo endurance racing engine.

Swiss race car constructor Peter Sauber built his first Group C car, the C6, in '82 in conjunction with composite material specialists Seger and Hoffmann. At the end of the season they parted company and while Seger and Hoffmann developed the 'Sehcar' from the Cosworth powered C6, Sauber produced a BMW engined car which was the only non-Porsche in the top 10 at Le Mans in '83. A Chevrolet powered version of the C7 was subsequently seen in IMSA in '84, during which season Sauber asked permission to use the Daimler-Benz wind tunnel at Unterturkheim, the marque's Stuttgart home.

The contact between Sauber and the Daimler-Benz R&D department led to consideration of a Mercedes V8 turbocharged Group C engine. Sauber had seen the potential of the all alloy, chain driven s.o.h.c., 16 valve M117 engine as the base for a powerful and reliable turbocharged Group C power plant. The M117 was the latest in a succession of Mercedes V8 engines stretching back to 1963. The original 6.3 (later 6.9) litre V8 had been followed in 1969 by a new generation 3.5 litre M116 V8 from which the M117 was directly descended.

The M116 had iron block and alloy heads with chain driven s.o.h.c. Its two valves per cylinder were offset 20 degrees from the vertical in a wedge-shaped combustion chamber surrounded by generous squish area, run in conjunction with a flat topped piston. Although the offset valves were set in parallel they were operated through finger cam followers which pivoted on spherical-headed adjuster studs. The M116 engine was taken out to 4.5 litres then, 10 years after its introduction, was replaced by the alloy block M117.

While the M117 generally followed the pattern of the iron block engine (retaining the wedge heads) the important difference was a massive weight saving in the order of 125kg. This was made possible through a new production technique offering a linerless block, as pioneered by General Motors with the famous Vega 2300 engine. The linerless block was diecast by the new 'Accurad' method in a new aluminium alloy, Reynolds A390, which combined good fluidity in the molten condition with a fine dispersion of silicon after heat treatment giving good bearing properties and ease of machining. After machining an electrochemical etching process was used to expose the hard silicon particles on the walls providing a wear resistant and oil retaining surface which was used in conjunction with an iron-plated piston skirt (reversing the usual combination of alloy piston on iron bore).

Though the production M117 engine was not turbocharged, the research engineers at Stuttgart were already familiar with the challenge of forced induction, having worked with turbocharged engines for 15 years. However, Damiler-Benz AG was not yet ready for a direct involvement in motor racing so the parts and technical information were supplied to Heini Mader who built the first twin turbo Mercedes Group C engine.

The project echoed that of Aston Martin, on behalf of which Tickford had toyed with a short lived Group C V8 turbo engine early in '84. The Mercedes challenger was a superficially similar, large capacity, lightly blown 90 degree V8. Likewise, it was essentially stock and consequently had a two plane crankshaft for smooth running. The two-plane configuration made for a very smooth engine at the expense of exhaust tuning potential. However, that was not a serious concern given forced induction and

the smooth, well balanced nature of the unit was considered idea for an endurance car.

The prototype engine first ran on the dyno around Christmas '34 and started track testing in March '85. Initially the head gasket gave problems but once the Stuttgart engineers had solved this it ran well. The solution was in a modified gasket and a stiffer head, the latter involving a modification to the casting which was carried through to the production car line.

The Mader engine benefitted from a dry sump, porting and camshaft work, increased water circulation, special heat resistant valves and oil sprayed pistons. Type 27 turbochargers were supplied by KKK and these were goverend by mechanical wastegates which were modified Porsche road car items. The appropriately revised induction system included air:air aftercoolers while injection and ignition were incorporated in the Porsche Group C-type Motronic M1.2 package which was supplied by Bosch. Daimler-Benz had worked closely with Bosch for many years.

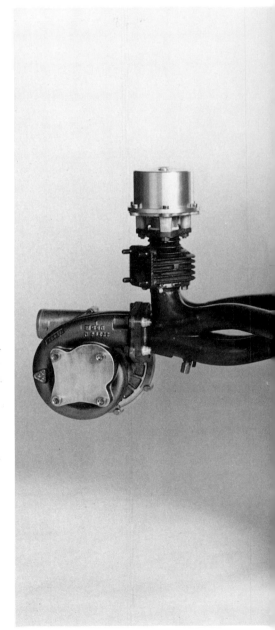

Rear end view of the Mercedes V8 M117 all alloy engine with twin KKK turbochargers. The unit ran a Motronic engine management system.

Together they had pioneered fuel injection for road car engines and engine management systems.

The Mader-assembled 5.0 litre Mercedes engine was pressurized to a maximum of 2.0 bar absolute in qualifying, at which power was in excess of 700bhp. Race boost was 1.8 bar absolute while for maximum power the drivers had to look no further than 6,600rpm.

Sauber went in at the deep end, the Mercedes-Sauber C8 debuting at Le Mans. Qualifying was encouraging until, warming up for a serious attempt to post a grid time, it took off over the brow after the Mulsanne kink. It somersaulted a couple of times and was wrecked, thankfully without injury to driver Nielson. Daimler-Benz kept faith with Sauber and a short, five-race programme was undertaken in '86, highlighted by victory in the wet at the Nurburgring, aided by the tremendous torque of the low revving, big displacement engine.

In the dry the Mercedes-Sauber was less impressive but with continuing engine development work and an improved chassis, the C9, in 1987 the package was a real contender. Again the season was only five races long and this time the highlight was pole at Francorchamps. For 1988 Daimler-Benz came out and gave the effort factory support for a full season and engines were supplied directly from Stuttgart. The commitment was immediately rewarded with a win at Jerez. Following a disappointing withdrawal from Le Mans in the wake of unexplained tyre blow outs, the team bounced back to win at the Norisring and Brno.

Over the Mader seasons the key engine developments were the introduction of Nikasil coated bores, a new lighter crankshaft, improved, higher efficiency turbochargers and a switch to the Motronic M1.7 engine management system offering more precise control of ignition and injection, plus electronic control of a new wastegate. In addition, a total of 20kg. was saved through lighter internals (including titanium con rods), a lighter flywheel, lighter ancillaries and lighter turbochargers. Even the camshafts were lightened, through a new form of construction.

With the more precise ignition control of the M1.7 system the compression ratio could be increased from an initial 8.0:1 to 8.5:1 while power was then officially 700bhp/7000rpm on the 1.9 bar absolute race setting. In qualifying almost 800bhp was extracted. Nevertheless, the base engine remained essentially a production item. M117 race engines were built from production castings which had been taken from the factory and sent to Mahle for a conventional Nikasil coating to be applied to the bores.

The linerless M117 block extended below the crankshaft axis to allow side as well as vertical bolting of the full-width main bearing caps. The four-bolt caps for the five bearings were of cast iron while the race engine's bespoke dry sump (attached via stock studs) was of magnesium and was designed to accept chassis loads. The engine was semi-stressed with loads also

The Pescarolo/Danner/Quester Sauber-Mercedes lasted only 86 laps of the 1986 Le Mans race, 25 more than its sister car. Both suffered engine failures.

fed into the heads. The ported alloy heads were attached by six bolts per cylinder and the valve gear was mounted directly on the head. An aluminium rocker cover was retained from the production engine.

The two-plane crankshaft ran in 64mm. diameter plain bearings supplied by Glyco and while lighter than standard was to the same design with the same balancing webs and journal sizes. An in-house production, it was of forged steel and was only polished, receiving no special treatment. As the production crankshaft, the race crank was fitted with a harmonic dampener but this was of a different design in view of the higher revs sought. It was supplied by Goetze. The flywheel was steel, attached by eight bolts and was sized to match a standard 7 1/4 inch clutch with a starter ring around it. The crankshaft was driven by titanium con rods through 48mm. diameter plain Glyco bearings.

The fully machined con rods were of I-section and were supplied by Pankel in Austria. At 170.5mm. eye to eye they were

a little longer than standard for a shorter, lighter piston. The Mahle piston was attached by a conventional steel gudgeon pin with circlips and was of the oil gallery type, fed by a single jet. The production head's wedge shaped combustion chamber was retained, the parallel valves inclined to one side with the plug reaching in on the other. The race engine differed only in a dish in the piston crown reducing the compression ratio from the stock 10.0:1.

The piston carried three cast iron rings, of which the top was chrome plated. The smaller, lighter piston carried smaller than standard rings. American supplier TRW provided the rings at Mahle's recommendation. The special head gasket resembled that of the production car and was supplied by German company Reinz. The head was fitted with Stellite seats for both inlet and exhaust valves which ran in bronze guides. The valves were steel with a Nimonic foot and on the exhaust side were sodium cooled. Dual steel springs were fitted under a titanium retainer.

The production valve gear was retained, with the finger cam followers reducing side loading compared to direct operation of the parallel valves by the cams. However, for the race engine the hydraulic piston atop which the follower's pivot was mounted to provide automatic adjustment was removed, replaced by a mechanically-adjusted stud. The only other modification was a specially hardened plate which was soldered to the top of the steel follower to form the cam working surface.

The camshaft had journals of large enough diameter to allow it to be inserted through bearing holes in aluminium shaft supports, five of which were were bolted to each head. The steel shaft ran directly in its supports and was of a newly devised built-up type produced by a Mahle subsidiary. The method was to produce the cam lobes and the journals separately then to slide them onto the tubular base shaft under a heat process. The resultant shaft was reckoned to be lighter and was less expensive to produce.

The camshafts were driven by a chain off a sprocket at the front of the crank. The double-row chain was a production item and was fitted with a tensioner. Between the front main bearing and the timing drive sprocket was another sprocket, this one to drive the oil pressure pump which was mounted inside the front cover. The scavenge pumps were mounted outside and were driven by a belt from a pulley on the nose of the crank. In fact there were two pullies, a second belt driving the water pump and alternator.

The water pump was set into the front cover in a central position while the scavenge pumps were to the left of the crankcase, the alternator to the right. Of the five scavenge pumps, three served the engine, two the turbos. Compared to the production engine the dry sump race unit had improved water circulation through enlarged channels - particularly in the head - with twice as much water in circulation.

The alternator was supplied by Bosch, which had developed a distributorless ignition system for the engine. Until mid '87 it ran with a conventional flywheel triggered Bosch CD system. However, with the M1.7 system, this was replaced by a multi-coil system, the coils triggered by the ECU which took impulses from the flywheel and a camshaft sensor. Rather than having a coil for each plug, one coil jointly served two cylinders and consequently each plug was fired twice per four stroke cycle. This was not, however, found to adversely affect performance. As for the production engine, the firing order was 1-5-4-8-6-3-7-2.

Fuel was injected into the ports rather than the inlet trumpets. The fuel injectors were screwed into the head, as on the production engine, one injector per cylinder. In spite of this arrangement atomization was considered adequate, "with the valve mostly responsible for atomization, anyhow", according to Development Engineer Withalm. Earlier the engine had run two injectors per cylinder with the second operating only at full throttle. However, improved injector design and improved control via the switch from M1.2 to M1.7 Motronic had allowed one to be dispensed with.

Two throttles were fitted, one just ahead of each entry to the plenum chamber, each turbocharger blowing through its own aftercooler. The inconel turbine turbochargers featured no trickery and had essentially remained unchanged throughout the engine's career. With the M1.7 system Daimler-Benz produced it own wastegates for electronic control throughout the rev range via the ECU. The driver remained in overall charge of the maximum boost pressure.

The Motronic ECU took readings, apart from those of the crankshaft and camshaft sensors, of charge air pressure as felt in the plenum, air and exhaust gas temperature, water temperature, oil temperature and pressure, fuel temperature and pressure and even turbocharger r.p.m. However, the system retained a plug-in EPROM, unlike the Zytek system used by Jaguar. It was used in conjunction with a telemetry system on race day, allowing the engineers to monitor temperatures and pressures. The map provided for the engine in 1988 was based on reference points at 500rpm and 0.1 bar intervals.

By 1988 Daimler-Benz had produced around 30 race engines. Each was reckoned to take two persons one week to strip and rebuild. There were no special qualifying engines but on 2.2 bar absolute qualifying power was rated as "almost 800bhp". Maximum revs were 7,000 but the driver was asked to observe a limit of 6,500 on race day, aside from overtaking. At the 1.9 bar absolute race setting torque was a massive 800n.m. at 4250rpm and the torque band was spread all the way from 3,000 to 6000rpm: sheer grunt was this unit's great strength.

Le Mans 1987 - Peter Sauber and crew attend the rapid Thackwell car. Constructor Sauber is holding the passenger door, while Thackwell awaits his turn.

MARCH NISSAN 86S

Overall victory in the 1985 Fuji 1000 kilometres against World Championship opposition in addition to successes in the American IMSA sports car series prompted the Nissan Motorsports division (NISMO) to commission a state-of-the-art chassis from March Engineering in which to field its victorious FB30 V6 engine at Le Mans in 1986.

March's aluminium honeycomb monocoque chassis, designed by Gordon Coppuck, incorporated classic wishbone front suspension with rocker arms and lower wishbones at the rear. Both ends were sprung by Koni coil spring/damper units and AP 13 inch disc brakes were mounted outboard with single four pot AP calipers and Ferodo pads. The bodywork was fashioned from carbon fibre and Kevlar with twin side mounted water radiators and twin air/air intercoolers ventilated by ducting through the doors. An oil cooler was mounted on top of the gearbox with its own duct behind the cockpit roof. Aerodynamically, the car featured a wedge shaped nose with minimal perforation and a short tail with a high, twin pillar mounted rear aerofoil. Sixteen inch Dymag wheels were shod with Bridgestone tyres.

The engine was a 60 degree V6 based on the 300ZX road car engine. Blown by two Garrett AiResearch turbochargers, the 2960 cc unit was reputed to produce more than 1000 bhp in qualifying trim. The block was of cast iron with aluminium heads, titanium being used extensively to keep the weight down. There were two over head camshafts per cylinder bank with two valves and one spark plug per cylinder. The engine had been developed in America by Electramotive of El Segundo, California and used Bosch fuel injectors and a Nissan EECP 16 bit microprocessor (as used on the Turbo 300ZX) in an Electramotive engine management system. In race trim power was quoted as 700 bhp at 8000 rpm.

Great potential was apparent in early testing but some concern was caused by the 'on-off switch' characteristics of the engine which seemed to lack a mid range. At the 1986 Le Mans test day the car was fifth fastest overall despite running only sporadically due to teething troubles.

For the race a single 86S chassis was entered along with an older 85G March production chassis which was over 100 kgs heavier than the purpose built car. In preparation for the meeting NISMO hired Keith Greene, one of the most experienced and respected of sports car racing team managers, with James Gresham of March sharing duties with him. On paper the team looked very strong. Alas, a catastrophic clash of cultures reduced the whole effort to a farce.

The Japanese drivers on the team ignored the directions of Greene, ludicrous scenes being enacted in the pits. In the race the new car was retired with an incurable engine vibration in the eighth hour while the 85G made it to the finish, in 17th place also having encountered engine problems.

The 86S returned in 1987 having been sold to the Japanese Tom Hanawa and was entered by Italya Sports. The car had an Electramotive engine and embarrassed the factory at the test weekend by lapping faster even though the works cars had new V8s at their disposal. In qualifying for the race the 86S was damaged when it was in collision with a slower car and hit the aramco. Rebuilt, it qualified slower than the works cars. Raced by Olofsson/Ferte/Gonin, the Swede got the car into tenth place in the early stages before Gonin crashed during the night. The V6 engine appeared again in '88 in a newer chassis.

NISSAN	
86S - 1986	60 degree V6
Honeycomb monocoque	3.0 litres
Suspension:	Iron block
wishbone front	Fuel injected
rocker arm rear	12 valves
Engine semi stressed	s.o.h.c.
March gearbox	Twin turbo
Ground effect car	700 b.h.p.

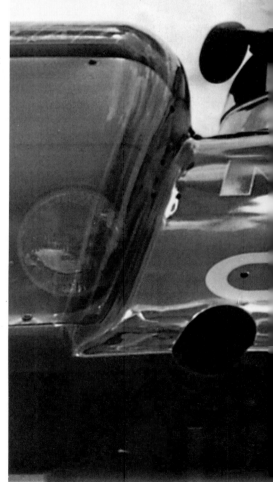

MARCH NISSAN R87E & R88E

At Le Mans in 1987 a new Nissan V8 engine made its European debut in a March chassis specially commissioned by Nissan. The engine was a 90 degree V8 with bore and stroke of 85 x 66mm. and a 3.0 litre displacement. Essentially, it was a conventional gear driven four valve alloy race engine but it did have a production based rocker system of valve actuation. Blown by two IHI turbochargers, it was reputed to produce 700 bhp on 0.8 bar boost.

The chassis was designed by Paul Bentley of March Engineering and featured an aluminium honeycomb monocoque reinforced by upper carbon fibre panelling. Magnesium bulkheads and uprights were featured. The V8 engine was mounted semi stressed in steel A-frames and with side mounted coolers the body outwardly resembled that of the Nissan RV86.

Nissan's two works entries recorded 17th and 20th qualifying times but were put out of the race by engine failures.

The engine was redrawn for 1988, though the basic configuration remained the same. The chassis was lengthened in the wheelbase and bodywork modifications were evident. This year the cars qualified 15th and 23rd for Le Mans and while a Japanese crewed example retired on Sunday morning with a broken exhaust valve that of Grice/Percy/Wilds made it home 14th in spite of many problems.

NISSAN	
R87E - 1987	90 degree V8
Honeycomb monocoque	3.0 litres
Suspension:	Alloy block
wishbone front	Fuel injected
rocker arm rear	32 valves
Engine semi stressed	d.o.h.c.
March gearbox	Twin turbo
Ground effect car	700b.h.p.

WM P76-86 PEUGEOT

The partnership of Gerard Welter (W) and Michel Meunier (M) produced its first racing car in 1969: as the partners were employees of Peugeot it was appropriate that it was a modified 204 saloon. With an engine tuned to produce 100bhp the team made its international debut in the Paris 1000kms. Further Peugeot-based projects followed and in 1976 a 2.7 litre V6 engined prototype was entered for the new GTP class at Le Mans. The aluminium 90 degree block engine produced 260bhp but the aluminium monocoque chassis failed early with a faulty fuel cell.

In 1977 an improved version of the WM-Peugeot appeared, the engine now fitted with a KKK turbocharger. The P77 was disqualified after repairs dropped it too far behind at the early morning distance check while the original P76 finished 15th. In 1978 a refined P78 appeared but this was destroyed in a big accident on Sunday morning which left the driver in hospital. The two earlier cars both retired with clutch and engine failures.

For 1979 three new chassis were entered but only one finished: 14th overall, it won the GTP class. For 1980 the cars were rebodied and twin KKK turbochargers lifted power to 500bhp. Fourth and 11th place finishes were achieved, overshadowed by the Rondeau victory. But Peugeot had been impressed and offered support for a four car team in 1981, this comprising two new P81s plus two P79/80s. Boutsen had a massive accident on the Mulsanne in one car while engine failure and a collision accounted for two more, the survivor finishing 14th.

In 1982 the ground effect underbody equipped WM P82 appeared and still with a characteristic narrow track and now 550bhp the model was clocked at 216mph in qualifying. The top speed was impressive but neither example finished. The following year's P83 boasted further aerodynamic changes and still more power - as high as 650bhp in qualifying. Both entries qualified in the top 12 but one retired with engine failure while the other was 16th after head gasket problems.

The WM P83s were uprated to 83B specification for the 1984 race and were hitting 226mph on the Mulsanne, fastest bar none. In the race team leader Roger Dorchy grabbed the lead on the first lap only to go off at Mulsanne corner when a brake snatched on lap three. The car was repairable but eventually succumbed to gearbox failure. The second car was retired around midnight with electrical problems.

For 1985 further engine development saw over 700bhp available in qualifying but in the race the three P83Bs were slower than in '84. Dorchy's lead car was crashed early on by Andruet when a tyre burst in the Mulsanne kink while another example with Rondeau among the drivers finished 17th. The third car was disqualified at post race scrutineering.

In 1986 the team ran one C1 and one C2 car, the latter having a two rather than four valve engine. The C1 83B retired with engine failure just before half distance but the two valve car finished 12th overall, second in C2. In 1987 the C1 car ran alongside the new P87 only for the cylinder head to crack in the first hour.

WM	PEUGEOT
P80 - 1980	90 degree V6
Aluminium monocoque	2.7 litres
Suspension:	Alloy block
wishbone front	Fuel injected
wishbone rear	32 valves
Engine stressed	d.o.h.c.
Hewland gearbox	Twin turbo
Flat bottom	500b.h.p.

WM P87/88 PEUGEOT

Just before the 1987 Le Mans race the WM team ran a straight line speed test on a closed section of autoroute and clocked 258 mph. The car under test was its new P87 chassis designed specifically to set a record 400 kph (250 mph) at Le Mans. Designed by Gerald Welter and Vincent Soulignac the car was based on regular WM running gear and had side mounted coolers fed from a central nose intake. The usual Peugeot twin turbo engine now had a Bosch engine management system and qualifying power was as high as 900 bhp.

The WM's aerodynamics were the product of testing at the St Cyr wind tunnel. An exceptionally smooth upper and lower body surface was made possible through ingenious internal airflow. The air from the nose entry was split into ducts for the coolers alongside the cockpit then, heated, was allowed to escape upwards through an opening at a low pressure area in the rear canopy. The car had a relatively shallow underwing and a rear wing designed to act as a trim tab. Although it looked long, the very clean design was actually shorter than the P86 in wheelbase.

Sadly engine problems in qualifying saw

the fastest official speed reading as 238 mph and poor fuel saw the car last only 13 laps of the race. In 1988 a second example, the P88, with minor revisions joined the original car and a full 3.0 litre capacity promised more engine power. However, both cars blew turbochargers in qualifying and both were in the pits within minutes of the start. This was particularly frustrating as the team was convinced it had exceeded 400 kph this year and in 1987 but that it had been let down by the official radar.

All was not lost, however, since the P88 was coaxed to run cleanly on Saturday evening and this time it was clocked by the official radar at 405 kph.

WM	PEUGEOT
P87 - 1987	90 degree V8
Aluminium monocoque	3.0 litres
Suspension:	Alloy block
wishbone front	Fuel injected
wishbone rear	32 valves
Engine stressed	d.o.h.c.
Hewland gearbox	Twin turbo
Ground effect car	+ 700b.h.p.

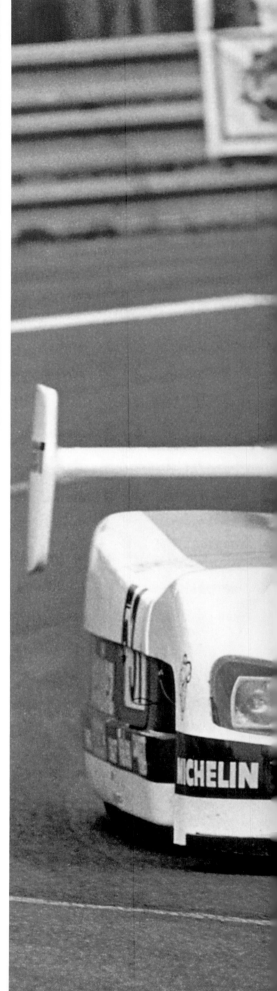

SHEER SPEED

Peugeot employees Gerard Welter and Michel Meunier had the idea of winning Le Mans using the boss' V6 engine. The boss lent moral support but by the time Porsche, Mercedes and Jaguar were all running works teams the aim had become impractical. So WM-Peugeot sought the accolade of King of the Mulsanne. Ian Bamsey investigates.

The roots of the WM project go back to the ACO's creation of the GTP class which invited a variety of engine options by fixing only a maximum consumption requirement of 35 litres per 100 km. Peugeot stylist Gerard Welter and Peugeot engineer Michel Meunier of 'WM' planned to field their own prototype propelled by the Peugeot 'PRV' V6 engine: the joint Peugeot-Renault-Volvo unit that had already inspired Renault's turbocharged V6. For its first, exploratory, outing in '76 WM ran its factory-assisted 2.7 litre unit unblown, breathing through three Weber carburettors. It nestled in a narrow track semi-monocoque coupe with a distinctive 'central backbone' chassis and conventional prototype running gear, including AP brakes and clutch, Michelin tyres and a ZF gearbox.

The team was staffed entirely by volunteer helpers, all personnel pursuing the project purely in their spare time. It didn't get its car home first time out but it did manage to clock up 15 hours steady running. For '77 Welter and Meunier sought more power, adding KKK turbocharging to a Bosch K-Jetronic fuel injected unit: this was another 'learning year', both entries falling by the wayside. There were three runners in '78, again without success, the last retirement a crash that destroyed the third chassis. For '79 Bosch road car injection gave way to the group's familiar Kugelfischer mechanical racing system and the team introduced its own four valve heads, designed in house by Meunier with detailing by fellow Peugeot engineer Michel Kreh, working spare time of course.

The engine was still based on a production four-bearing block, to which had been added side bolting for the main bearing caps (these spanning the width of the lower crankcase). The side bolts had been introduced by WM in '76 to avoid cracking and were subsequently adopted by Peugeot as a standard feature. Unlike the production engine, the WM version was dry-sumped and gradually the team was phasing in its own parts: crank, con rods, pistons, and so forth. It cooled each piston by a single spray to the underside of the crown.

The new d.o.h.c. four valve head called for an alloy casting, with separate tappet block, which was produced outside of Peugeot and it was still chain driven, WM positioning a second gear behind the upper production sprocket to turn the gear on each camshaft.

In '79 WM again ran three cars, building a new 'P79' and upgrading the other two to the same specification. This year the volunteer squad brought one home, 14th overall, and first in GTP, Raulet and Mamers at the controls.

For 1980 the rear bodywork was modified following wind tunnel tests at the St. Cyr fixed floor facility used by the Renault and Ligier race teams and, helped by its characteristically narrow track, the WM clocked the impressive Mulsanne speed of 217mph: fastest of all. The engine was now rated 500bhp on 2.2 bar absolute in race trim and the Thorigny, near Paris, based team was delighted to achieve a fourth placed finish for its Frequelin/Dorchy car. One of its other two entries also finished, placed 11th.

Peugeot was delighted, too, and helped with engine modifications which included a new front plate and cam covers allowing the unit to be run fully stressed. The bore was taken out from the traditional 88mm. to 91mm., while retaining the production 73mm. stroke (for 2850cc). No less than four chassis were readied, allowing the luxury of a spare car and Mulsanne speed went up to 223mph. Alas, shunts took out two cars while the third could manage no better than 14th following a wishbone failure.

The two remaining cars were run in '82

and '83 without success (only one finish: 16th in '83) then the team was forced into liquidation by a change in the French tax laws affecting charitable organisations. Its assets were acquired by regular driver Dorchy, owner of a garage in Beauvais. He kept the operation, now called 'SECATEVA' and 'profit making', alive at his premises (20 Rue des Moulins) and Welter was able to produce an updated model: a refined version of the existing car with longer wheelbase and improved aerodynamics for higher top speed. The team was even able to produce a third chassis.

Engine development was now in the hands of DMC: Denis Mathiot Competition, a small 'service course' operation based at Lagny near Paris. Mathiot introduced a digital electronic control to make the Kugelfischer injection cam responsive to revs as well as boost and throttle opening. Race power was officially quoted as 600bhp/7000rpm with torque a maximum of 62m./kg. at 6000rpm.

Kevlar bodywork was used for the first time (bringing weight down to 825kg.) but the small frontal area 'P84' design was still flat bottomed and this assisted the quest for speed on the Mulsanne. Dorchy used that speed (over 220mph/ officially as high as 363k.p.h. (227mph)) to pass Wollek's leading Lancia the first time down the chute - only to half spin at Mulsanne corner with brakes too heavily biased to the rear. Undaunted, he repeated the feat on lap three - and this time speared into the barrier. Repairs cost an hour, then the car retired with gearbox failure. The sister car lost its engine.

For '85 two of three (essentially unmodified) entries ran a stronger Hewland gearbox while a higher compression ratio pushed power over 600bhp. This year one car crashed out (tyre failure in the kink) while the others finished well out of the reckoning. However, for '86 SECATEVA was able to move out of Dorchy's garage, back to Thorigny (132 Route de Claye). Both remaining cars were run and while one retired (engine), the other, running in C2 with an engine reduced to 2650cc and only two valves per cylinder, finished 12th overall, third in class.

Running in C2 was indicative of hopelessness of outright victory as Le Mans became ever more costly thanks to the increasing level of Group C competition. However, WM had already planned a realistic target: Project 400. In '86 the team's C1 car had clocked 371kph - a faster speed than any previously recorded on the three and a half mile long Mulsanne straight. In 1971 Jackie Oliver had gone over 380kph in a long tail Porsche 917 but that had not been officially clocked. Consequently the old 'record' had been the 363kph recorded by the team in 1984 - that beat the previous best set by a Renault with special 'bubble' cockpit

172

canopy in 1978 by a mere 1kph.

However, 371kph wasn't the fastest clocking of '86: the Joest Porsche driven by Ludwig had gone 374kph to steal the record from WM. The French team didn't mearly plan to regain its supremacy of the Linge Droit des Hunaudieres, it aimed to field the first car to exceed 400kph in the course of a race.

The challenge was to reduce drag without dangerous loss of stability. Drag reduction makes a car more sensitive to lateral aerodynamic forces and the problem intensifies as speed increases, as Porsche found to its cost with its early long tail 917 coupes. Porsche set out with a drag co-efficient of 0.33 for its original 4.5 litre, 550bhp streamliner, predicting 236mph on the Mulsanne. However, unlike the marque's earlier low drag small capacity cars this model proved undriveable without additional downforce, which cost drag. The ultimate 917LH of 1971, a Le Mans special that was adequately stable, had the drag co-efficient of 0.36. That was still a remarkable by race car standards: for example, the standard 917K had a co-efficient of 0.464.

WM set out to achieve a co-efficient of 0.3, some ten points lower than its regular flat bottom car. The project was directed by Welter, a man responsible for some remarkable Peugeot styling exercies including the striking Quastar, star of the 1984 Paris Motor Show. Aside from Meunier, the other prime movers were Team Manager Gerard Clabeaux and WM's chassis specialist Vincent Soulignac, a Peugeot research engineer from 9am. - 5pm. Peugeot agreed to sponsor wind tunnel time for the team and essential backing for what would have to be an all-new chassis came from Michelin, Valeo and Heuliez.

Over a period of four months the WM principals spent every Sunday at the St. Cyr wind tunnel evaluating 1/10th scale models, testing 25 different configurations on each occasion. The final product was based on a wheelbase of 2500mm. rather than the 2320mm. of the superseded car with an overall length of 4490mm. compared to 4120mm. and a full 2000mm. width as against only 1780mm. While the track was a little wider, the extra body width was primarily to provide considerable front wheel arch overhang.

The idea of the overhang was to allow partial fairing of the front wheels and to reduce interference between the flow along the sides of the car and the air whipped around by wheel rotation. The rear wheels were fully faired-in. The WM P87 was not designed as a flat bottom car but had ground effect venturi tunnels and a low set full width rear wing as an integral feature of the low drag design. According to the setting of the wing the drag co-efficient was an astonishing 0.26-0.28: first target achieved.

The P87 chassis was an evolution of the existing equipment with aluminium sheet and honeycomb monocoque retaining the distinctive 'backbone' running between the seats. The car ran on 16" diameter front wheels, 19" diameter rears stopped by AP four pot brakes. The conventional wishbone suspension incorporated Koni gas dampers. The fully stressed V6 engine was switched from KKK to Garrett twin turbochargers for better matching and more boost (each feeding through an air:air aftercooler) and benefitted from a Bosch Motronic engine management system. Maximum boost was 2.5 bar absolute with maximum revs of 8,200rpm and a power output of 850bhp.

The one-off P87 was finished just in time for the Le Mans test day on May 17 and new car teething problems saw the machine unable to string laps together. However, lead driver Dorchy (veteran of eight 24 hour races with the team) expressed himself pleased with the car and reckoned there was plenty more to come after setting a 356kph best on the Mulsanne. Subsequently the team spent a couple of days sorting the machine on the Bugatti circuit then, on June 4, ran it on a six kilometer stretch of unopened St. Quentin - Rheims autoroute near the town of Laon. Francois Migault took the controls for a single run on a moist road surface under threatening dark clouds and in front of French TV cameras. He watched the digital speed read out climb to 390k.p.h. then concentrated on driving.. the machine flashed through WM's police radar at 416kph "It was easy, the car felt very safe", Migault reported.

Subsequently Dorchy ran 404kph over the course of two days at Michelin's Clermont Ferrand test track where there was a one kilometer straight followed by a fast turn. In total the car clocked up 1000km. prior to the race, experiencing no major problems. Alas, turbocharger and electronic problems spoilt Wednesday qualifying at Le Mans but there was more success

the following day: 407kph on the team's radar. The official radar, however, recorded only 381kph as Dorchy howled through at 8000rpm on full boost at 7.38pm.

Dorchy reported the car's full bore behaviour "acceptable, but not comfortable", as it drifted across the road somewhat (which it hadn't on the autoroute) and found it necessary to lift slightly for the kink. He vowed to go for 400kph on race day but that plan was thwarted by engine malady, later blamed on the low octane rating of the fuel supplied by the organisers, which also caused the Porsche runners problems...

WM was convinced that its 407kph clocking was genuine but had to be content with its new record of 381kph. By the Monday evening after the event it was working on its 1988 challenge, for which a second streamliner was built. This had a similar chassis with modified front and rear suspension, the rear suspension redesign carried over to the P87 and allowing lower but wider diffuser tunnels. The front suspension modification was one of geometry and in addition the new car had a strengthened monocoque. It had an identical external form but the body was revised under the skin, helping improve downforce without spoiling the drag coefficient while improving cooling. Air was collected for the radiators at the front of the nose, was ducted over the wheels and either side of the cockpit and was allowed to escape into a low pressure area in the top of the rear deck.

Engine modification for '88 included a 93mm. bore and at 2.8 bar and maximum revs of 8200rpm. Dorchy was summoning approximately 910bhp. Qualifying saw him clock another 407kph pass based on information recorded by the ECU log, casting further suspicion over the official radar, which was reluctant to acknowledge anything much over 380kph. However, Dorchy tried again on race day and was rewarded with an official 405kph: mission accomplished.

Record de vitesse pour la W.M. de François Migault

L'autoroute à 416 km-h

Record battu ! Le pilote manceau François Migault a atteint au volant de sa W.M. la vitesse fabuleuse de 416 km-heure L'événement s'est déroulé, hier, sur l'autoroute de l'Est, sur un tronçon situé entre Saint-Quentin et Reims. Une performance de tout premier plan pour cette « P. 87 » toute nouvelle, repassée en soufflerie cet hiver et dont la puissance du P.R.V. double turbo impressionne. Voilà un exploit qui devrait faire beaucoup de bruit dans le monde de la course, à quelques jours seulement des « 24 Heures du Mans ». (EN 18)

● Les 13 et 14 juin prochains, l'équipe W.-M. de Gérard Clabeaux ne sera pas forcément dans le rétroviseur pour les pilotes des « Porsche » et « Jaguar ».

PORSCHE 936 JOEST & KREMER PORSCHE CK5

Porsche did not make customer versions of its 956 racer available until the second season of Group C. Thus for 1982 regular Porsche entrants Joest and Kremer built their own Porsche-based Group C specials. The Joest car was a converted 936 spaceframe Group 6 car and was thus powered by a 2.1 litre flat six turbo engine: blown by twin KKK turbochargers the unit was of the two valve variety. To conform to Group C requirements the car was clothed in a new coupe body and this was produced in g.r.p. by Zimmerman of Cologne. For Le Mans a tail extension was added with a full width aerofoil and the engine was switched for a two valve 935 unit displacing 2.8 litres and producing 560 bhp on 1.3 bar boost.

In the hands of Wollek the car was fast qualifying third, beaten only by two works 956s. Wollek and the Martin brothers looked set to finish third overall, too, only for piston failure to stop the car in the 23rd hour. In 1983 the car re-appeared at Le Mans as a back up to Joest's 956 but was an early retirement with fuel pump failure. Three years on it returned yet again, now owned by an amateur team. Nevertheless, it finished a commendable sixth overall.

Kremer's CK5 chassis was powered by a similar 935 engine and likewise was based on a Porsche spaceframe. It sported a stylish body distinguished by a ground hugging nose and a dorsal fin which gave central support to the rear aerofoil. A diffuser was fitted behind the engine to create a measure of negative pressure under the flat bottom.

The CK5 arrived at Le Mans in 1982 completely untested yet qualified eighth. Sadly, a head gasket blew after less than two hours. The car re-appeared in 1983 now owned by the Richard Cleare team and Kremer had also produced a second example which boasted larger rear wheels to allow a larger diffuser to be fitted. Alas, both retired before half distance. The Cleare car was stranded out on the circuit with a flat battery while the works car suffered another head gasket failure.

KREMER	PORSCHE
CK-5 - 1982	Boxer 6
Alloy spaceframe	2.7 litres
Suspension:	Alloy blocks
wishbone front	Fuel injected
wishbone rear	12 valves
Engine unstressed	s.o.h.c.
Porsche gearbox	Twin turbo
Ground effect car	+ 500 b.h.p

COUGAR
C12/20/22
PORSCHE

Having run DFL engined cars at Le Mans between 1982 and '84, Yves Courage and his Le Mans based team produced a new design for the 1985 season to be powered by a Porsche 956 engine. The monocoque chassis was designed by Courage and had an aluminium honeycomb tub. The engine was mounted as a semi stressed member and was tilted upwards as in the 956/962 chassis to provide clearance for the underwing. Cooling was by coolers mounted in the flanks while the body shape was the work of Marcel Hubert who had been the aerodynamic consultant for the 1978 Le Mans winning Renault. His design incorporated bulbous front wheel arches, a nose splitter and a high twin strut mounted rear wing, the overall appearance reminiscent of the victorious Renault.

With 650 bhp on tap and an effective shape the car was fastest on the Mulsanne at Le Mans in '85, recording 231 mph. However, handling shortcomings meant it lined up only 19th. In the race the C12 ran in the top ten until pushed off the track. Delayed by the damage repairs, the car finished 20th in the hands of Courage/de Cadenet/Yvon.

In 1986 the C12 re-appeared at Le Mans with a new body design which re-directed air through the doors to the radiators and intercoolers leaving the flanks unopen. Squarer front arches had also been adopted. Yet the car could now manage only 217 mph. After losing doors, it finished the race 18th.

Le Mans 1987 saw a new C20 chassis with a similar monocoque base, though featuring a titanium floor panel. However, the wheelbase was 20mm. longer and the car was around 30 kg. lighter. The body was based on that seen in 1986 with the wing lower. Fitted with a Motronic engine the car was clocked at 223 mph and started sixth on the grid. Fuel pump problems caused some delays yet third overall was achieved.

In 1988 the C20 returned to Le Mans and crashed in qualifying. Rebuilt, it started the race 17th only to catch fire in the pits, which wiped out its electrical system. Completing a miserable race for the team, a new C22 design with a fully water cooled engine, revised aerodynamics and pull rod front suspension was destroyed in a high speed accident.

COUGAR	PORSCHE
C12 - 1985	Boxer 6
Honeycomb monocoque	2.6 litres
Suspension:	Alloy blocks
wishbone front	Fuel injected
rocker arm rear	24 valves
Engine semi-stressed	d.o.h.c.
Porsche gearbox	Twin turbo
Ground effect car	650b.h.p.

MARCH & GRID PORSCHE

In spite of the liquidation of Grid Racing, an SA2 chassis propelled by a 2.9 litre turbocharged Porsche 935 engine was entered for the 1984 Le Mans race by CAM Racing and was run by Charles Ivey, the Porsche specialist. The chassis was a development of the Cosworth powered SA1, based on the same aluminium honeycomb monocoque with rocker arm front and rear suspension and the engine fitted as a semi-stressed member. There were bodywork alterations including lengthened nose booms which carried the front mounted aerofoil, surface ducting for the engine and a strut mounted rear wing. Qualified 29th, the car was the first retirement when it ran out of fuel after just one hour of racing.

Another British built Porsche special was one of the dark horses of the 1985 race. This was the semi-works March 84G-Porsche entered by Kreepy Krauly Racing and powered by the more potent 956 engine. The chassis was similar to that which had carried a Buick engine the previous year. Hopes were high since in GTP guise the car had won the Daytona 24 Hours against strong opposition. It had been converted from GTP to Group C specification by DJ Racing of Indianopolis, the conversion including the fixing of a flat 80 x 100 cm panel onto the ground effect underside. This was rejected by the Le Mans scrutineers and part of the first qualifying session was forfeited while adjustments were made.

The conversion to Group C specification allowed the fitting of an unrestricted Porsche turbo engine and the regular 2.65 litre 956 unit was employed. The car also carried 956 gearbox and rear suspension while the engine sat flat rather than tilted as in a 956 chassis due to the different underbody requirements of the GTP based car. Plagued by qualifying problems, then suspension failures and engine management

gremlins in the race, the car finished a disappointing 22nd overall.

The machine was bought after Le Mans by Cosmik Racing and it appeared again at Le Mans in 1986 only to be crashed by a French 'Rent-a-driver' during qualifying. Repaired, it got into the top 20 just after half distance only to retire, an electrical failure stopping the engine. At the same race an ex-John Kalagan March 85G was run in the IMSA GTP category by Richard Cleare Racing. It could thus run the original March GTP underbody but it was confined to a single turbocharger, two valve fully air cooled flat six engine. Also damaged in practice, the GTP car was more fortunate in the race finishing 14th overall and winning its class.

GRID	PORSCHE
S2 - 1984	Boxer 6
Honeycomb monocoque	2.6 litres
Suspension:	Alloy blocks
rocker arm front	Fuel injected
rocker arm rear	24 valves
Engine semi-stressed	d.o.h.c.
Porsche gearbox	Twin turbo
Ground effect car	650b.h.p.

PORSCHE 956

This was Porsche's first monocoque car, first ground effect car. It positioned its coolers either side of the new sheet aluminium tub where they were fed through door ducts from the air passing around the sides of the cockpit superstructure. The underwing swept up behind the mandatory flat bottom area with the engine tilted upwards to accommodate it. The flat six unit employed was of the four valve type with water cooled heads as developed for the 935 programme and the 2.65 litre displacement of an abandoned Indy Car project was adopted. With Bosch mechanical injection and CD ignition and twin KKK turbochargers supplying 1.3 bar boost the power output was in the region of 620 bhp. The unit had been proven in the 1981 Le Mans winning spyder chassis.

For the 1982 Le Mans race boost was a careful 1.1 bar and the all important transmission was a new Porsche five speeder with syncromesh, as usual. At the rear the spring/dampers were mounted over the gearbox and were operated by rocker arms. The car made its debut at Silverstone in 1982 then three works machines were entered for Le Mans. These had extended tails retaining a fin-mounted rear wing. Although 60kg over the Group C weight limit, the new Porsche coupes took the top two grid positions and scored a crushing one - two - three in the race headed by Ickx/Bell.

In 1983 Porsche sold customer versions while racing its works cars with lighter monocoque and bodywork, revised front suspension and a Bosch Motronic engine management system. Three works entries were backed by eight customer cars at Le Mans and the Schuppan/Haywood/Holbert factory car narrowly beat the Ickx/Bell sister car. Third was the Kremer car of Andretti father and son and Alliot and only a Sauber-BMW in ninth place stopped a 956 clean sweep of the top 10 places. The third works car was the only 956 retirement with a broken piston.

The factory sold '83 works-spec. customer cars for '84 and boycotted Le Mans

for political reasons. Nevertheless, 16 Porsches raced, many to the newer spec and some with team modifications such as a one piece underbody. However, the winning Joest team shunned the Motronic system. Its Ludwig/Pescarolo car was delayed early on by a fuel pressure problem and dropped to 30th overall yet fought back to lead from the 17th hour. This year eight of the top 10 finishers were 956s, second overall Rondeau/Paul/Henn in the latter's car, third Hobbs/Streiff/van der Merwe for the Fitzpatrick team.

By 1985 the works had the 962C but nine 956s were entered including the '84 winner which did the double, leading from the third hour to the finish. Its performance perplexed even the factory team. Ludwig/Barilla/'Winter' were the victorious drivers while second were Palmer/Weaver in another 956. This version, however, a 'special' built by the Richard Lloyd team around a replacement honeycomb monocoque.

1986 was the last year in which the pedals-ahead-of-front-axle 956 design was legal and seven were entered, with the Joest chassis no. 117 looking for a hat trick. That was on the cards until a prolonged pace car period played havoc with the engine which ran its bearings. This year the best placed 956 was third: another Joest car driven by Follmer/Morton/Miller.

PORSCHE	
956 - 1982	Boxer 6
Aluminium monocoque	2.6 litres
Suspension:	Alloy blocks
wishbone front	Fuel injected
rocker arm rear	24 valves
Engine semi-stressed	d.o.h.c.
Porsche gearbox	Twin turbo
Ground effect car	620b.h.p.

WINNING MACHINE

The Porsche 956 was built to win and win it did. With mechanical precision. From 1982 until 1987 the model and the similar 962 derivative held an iron grip upon Le Mans. 956 authority John Allen discussed the philosophy, the design and the trend of subsequent development of the original car with the engineers that made the legend.

One of the most important ingredients for a gripping story is struggle. All the really fascinatinig tales about racing cars deal with the designers' and the drivers' efforts to make the thing go faster (or even merely fast) while keeping it on the ground, making it go around corners without tipping over, slowing it down when approaching those corners, providing it with a passable level of acceleration and top speed, and screwing it together tightly enough so that it can cover the necessary distance without falling apart. On that basis, the Porsche 956 story can hardly be described as an epic; from the moment it first turned a wheel, it was as essentially right as any racing car can ever hope to be.

The 956 was a brand new car for a brand new formula, Group C, the replacement for Group 6, and the all-new championship the task of which was to revive the flagging fortunes of sports car racing. Porsche had been faithful to sports car racing since 1949, so it was inconceivable that they would not respond to the challenge of Group C.

The most striking feature of the Porsche 956 was its chassis; for the first time, Porsche built a monocoque for a racing car. There were several reasons for doing this, but the most important was perhaps the least obvious. It was clear that the provision of ground effect aerodynamics, which had never previously been incorporated into a Porsche, would benefit from the use of a monocoque. This method of construction did away with the mass of tubing which is anathema to ground effect, making the incorporation of air-tunnels virtually impossible; equally the monocoque can be made substantially stiffer than tube-frame chassis, with commensurate improvements in handling and roadholding. Yet another advantage of the monocoque is that production tolerances are usually less than for spaceframes, and Porsche's monocoques

Silverstone. 1982: debut of the 956 in the hands of Ickx and Bell. The car immediately set a new standard for Group C.

are not twisted, as some of its spaceframes were found to be.

Porsche wanted to build a monocoque, because it had not done so before, and the technical aspects of the project appealed. The most fundamental reason did, however, relate to the embryo Group C's then unfinalised rules, which at the time specified a degree of driver-protection which could not have been met with a tubular chassis. In the event, the rules as finally decreed were not as demanding in this respect as the draft regulations had been, so the extra safety inherent in a monocoque turned out to be a bonus rather than a feature made mandatory by the rules.

The first example of the chassis was constructed purely for experimental purposes, and was not intended to become part of a car. Although it followed the general outline of the definitive chassis, it was simpler in many respects, and lacked many of the detail fittings found on production chassis. The material used in the construction of all examples of the 956 was plain sheet aluminium, this being chosen largely because of the time pressures which then existed. Design work commenced in August 1981, work beginning on the first car in November, with the prototype reaching the test track by March 1982, although it missed the first round of the 1982 World Endurance Championship in April.

Although the chassis was satisfactory from the outset, many minor changes were made both to lighten it and to stiffen it, although throughout its career Porsche made no attempt to go for more exotic materials, such as aluminium honeycomb, let alone carbon-fibre. At Weissach it is believed that the privately-made honeycomb chassis, which from late 1984 some teams began to use as replacements for the factory product, are no stiffer than the official monocoque, and by mid-1988 Porsche still had no definite plans to produce such a chassis itself. One ultra-lightweight sheet aluminium tub was built but it was used for test purposes only, and never found its way into production.

Ever since Porsche drew the disastrous shape of the first 917, and had to suffer the indignity of seeing outsiders help transform that shape into one of the most effective sports-racers ever, Porsche has left no aerodynamic matters to chance; the result of intensive work in this field has meant that all Porsches are invariably aerodynamically sound by the time they first reach the racetrack. The 956's shape incorporated several features new to Porsche. The extreme nose was devoid of the usual intake for oil-cooling air, and was thus very clean, containing only three small ducts, one of which fed the cockpit, the others providing airflow to the brakes.

The oil radiators were removed from the

customary position in the nose, and were re-sited alongside the rear bulkhead of the monocoque, sharing space with the intercoolers and cylinder head coolant radiators. Grouping all the radiators together not only allowed the nose to be kept sleek, but also helped greatly in the car's balance; they were well within the 956's wheelbase, where they would have minimal effect on the car's behaviour. They could also be fed with air from only two openings, one in the top of each door. Initially, these intakes were formed in the shape of NASA ducts, but early tests at Paul Ricard found the water temperature becoming too high, and showed that the ducts were insufficient for the volume of cooling air required. As a stop gap measure, simple rectangular openings were provided instead, but these proved to be so successful that, although it was intended that they be improved eventually, they remained unchanged until the advent of the 1988 season, when the arrival of the

Model of the projected shape of the 956 to allow wind tunnel evaluation of its aerodynamics. Porsche used fixed floor rather than superior rolling road testing yet got the overall shape about right.

new Motronic 1.7 engine management system required changes to the radiator layout as a whole.

Body panels were constructed of Kevlar, fibreglass and aluminium. The undersides of the two optional noses were given aerofoil section, to aid downforce; on their upper surfaces, the two noses had almost identical contours, but the undersurfaces were quite different, so as to provide differing levels of downforce to match the characteristics of the two optional tails. The noses were detachable, a new feature for racing Porsches, and clearly an advantage as they permitted easy removal and replacement of damaged sections. Two types of tail were built and tested before the car raced, both designs being intended for very different purposes. The shorter of the two tails featured high vertical fins and a transverse wing, while on the longer tail the fins were lower, and were also joined by a transverse wing. Overall lengths of all 956s (and their later developments, the 962s) were identical, irrespective of the type of tail fitted; although the tails themselves were of different lengths, the overhang of the fins was changed accordingly, resulting in no difference in overall dimensions.

The purpose of the long tail was to reduce drag, which it did dramatically, as well as to reduce downforce. Obviously the major circuit where this would be an advantage was Le Mans, where the fuel consumption rules of Group C were likely to be a particular problem, due to the high average speeds achievable there. It was also intended that the long tail would be used at other circuits, and the rear of the car was engineered so that a switch between the two types of tail, plus swapping of other appropriate components such as shock-absorbers, springs, floor-panel and nose, could be accomplished in around two hours.

Wheels were one-piece castings by Speedline. At the front they were originally 11 inches wide, and 16 inches in diameter, and made specifically for Dunlop Denloc tyres; Porsche had always worked with Dunlop, and there was no question of another make of tyre being used. In the early stages it was found that the front rims were too narrow; this manifested itself in a minor understeer problem, but the real difficulty was one of tyre wear, it being relatively unusual for a mid-engine car to suffer heavy wear of the front tyres. This largely arose because the 956's downforce was much greater than that of its predecesor, the 936, but the design had not sufficiently allowed for this. Experiments were carried out using the easily adjustable modular wheels made by BBS, and these resulted in an initial width increase to 12 inches, then a second and final increase to the 13

inches which was still in use in 1988.

The wheels were fitted with external plates incorporating internal fan blades, designed to draw air across the brakes and out through the outer face of the wheel. These fans were very effective, but in the early days some temperature-measuring tests produced results which suggested that the fans were only of value when used on the front wheels. This information was then disseminated to customers using the cars, and both works and private entrants abandoned rear-wheel fans. Later, the tests were repeated, and it was discovered that the original results were wrong, probably due to the temperature sensors being damaged; consequently, the revised information was passed to users, and 956's re-appeared with fans fitted on their rear wheels.

The first one-fifth scale wind-tunnel model of the car was sufficient to provide accurate information concerning the balance, drag and downforce of the Le Mans version of the car, so that when the Le Mans configuration was subjected to one day's testing at Circuit Paul Ricard, to reset the springs and dampers as appropriate, no other changes were required, and the car's shape was considered correct right from the start. Indeed, the single day's testing at Ricard prompted Derek Bell to say that he preferred the Le Mans version of the car to the short-tail sprint model. Apparently the lower downforce of the Le Mans car made it considerably easier to slide, and so it did not require the precision handling which the sprint car needed. The steering, too, was better on the Le Mans car. Although both versions were actually the same mechanically, drivers did complain of rather heavy steering on the short-tail model. This was in part due to the high level of downforce being generated, so the problem righted itself automatically in the Le Mans 956. It was, however, subsequently the subject of some modification, and both castor angle

and wheel offset were changed in a successful bid to lighten the steering effort.

The engine of the 956 was a carry-over from the 936/81 which in 1981 had raced, and won, at Le Mans. It was thus one of the few proven parts of the car. Porsche had endured considerable problems (notably with cylinder-head cooling) with the 2.1-litre version of its turbocharged flat-six, as installed in earlier 936s, and so it was decided to produce a new engine for 1981. Basically, this consisted of the block of the 2.1-litre, but with heads derived from those of the 2.8-litre type 935, the whole having much in common with the version intended orignally for Indianapolis, and retaining the Indy maximum capacity of 2.65 litres. Cylinders were air-cooled, but the heads were cooled by water; dimensions were very much oversquare, with a bore of 92.3mm and a stroke of 66.0mm. The engine was turbocharged, using a pair of KKK K-26 360 turbochargers, and was rated 620BHP at 8200rpm; power outputs for turbocharged cars have very little relevance, for the output can so easily be changed, at the cost of increased fuel consumption, at the turn of an in-car knob. The engine and gearbox assembly was set nose-down in the chassis, at an angle of 5 ; this gave additional clearance for the air-tunnels, and, as a side benefit, ensured that the drive shaft angle would never be excessive.

Contemporary reports stated that the gearbox installed in the 956 had previously been tested in a 944 at the 1981 Le Mans race, but there appears to be no substance to this story, which Porsche denies. The gearbox was developed specifically for the 956, and since no decision as to the buildinig of the 956 had been made until after Le Mans that year, then the gearbox cannot have been tried out beforehand.

Between the gearbox, and the engine was a long spacer, housing the clutch. Originally cast in magnesium, the spacer incorporated a hatch through which the clutch could be removed, thus permitting clutch changes without the need to dismantle the rear end of the car, a problem which afflicts many mid-engined sports-racers. The clutch housing was later recast in aluminium, which increased its weight by some three to four kilos, but it also increased substantially its stiffness, which was the object of the exercise. The large-gauge steel tubing which connected the rear of the chassis to the transmission was also strengthened, both by using heavier material and additional struts; naturally, this added weight to the car, which in its original form scaled approximately 830kg, some 30kg more than Group C's 1982 minimum weight.

Rear end of the original 956. Note tilted drivetrain, bellhousing-cum-spacer, A-frame support for the rear end (to avoid channeling all chassis loads through the engine) and generous provision for underbody diffuser tunnels.

Construction of Porsche's first monocoque chassis. Porsche used a plain sheet aluminium tub whereas rivals sought added rigidity through employment of honeycomb sandwich.

At the front, the suspension was conventional double-wishbone, with outboard coil-spring/damper units, the springs being tapered titanium. Rear suspension was unusual, with upper rocker-arms and spring/damper units being inboard so as to keep the space alongside the gearbox clear, and thus allow for more airflow through the ground-effect tunnels. Use of small diameter steel driveshafts helped in this respect. Brakes were ventialed both axially and radially, but at some circuits (notably Le Mans) it is not unknown for the ventilation to be radial only; drilling through the discs can cause cracking, and in cool weather at Le Mans the discs can often run cool enough without such drilling being necessary.

Drivers consider the cockpit to be reasonably comfortable, although it was made as small as was permitted by Group C rules. To ventilate the interior, sliding side windows were fitted on early cars, but as a weight-saving measure the sliding panels were later abandoned, and replaced by three or more holes cut, in a vertical row, into the plexiglass. Later versions (962s) racing in the USA were some-

Boost control knob, operating wastegate settings for the twin KKK turbos. Pressure in the twin plenum chambers needed to go no higher than 2.2 bar absolute.

times equipped with ice-boxes, fitted in the wide side sills of the bodywork, and providing iced water to drivers' cool-suits. The same bodywork side boxes housed battery, pneumatic air-jacks, and turbocharger and engine management boxes.

Group C was very much a fuel-orientated formula, and at the first event contested by the prototype 956, the car faced severe fuel problems. The Silverstone race in 1982 was run over 6-hours rather than the more usual 1000km, so that the distance the 956 actually covered in that time, 1,118km, turned out to be more than it could cope with happily on the 1000km fuel allowance. There were no problems with fuel allowance on the Le Mans cars that year, for a combination of reasons. In the first place, most of the opposition was decimated early on, leaving the 956s to run at a comfortable pace; another major factor was the low downforce bodywork, which cut drag considerably. Boost pressure was kept low (only 1.1-bar gauge during the race), and corners were taken in top gear wherever possible. Although the theoretical allowance for Le Mans was only 2600 litres, 4.33 times that allowed for 1000km events, the winning 956 managed to cover no less than 4,899km, just 4.38 times the distance covered at Silverstone.

The three brand-new 956s which arrived at Le Mans scrutineering were all in long-tail configuration, and had been fitted with digital fuel readouts to allow the drivers to monitor their cars' consumption. Le Mans

cars usually are heavier than their spring-racing equivalents, because of additional equipment carried on board, and the 956s were no exception in this respect. The cars carried tool boxes, which included alternator drive belts, these having in the past proved to be most valuable. Although cars ought to be able to cover one lap to reach the pits, whilst using only battery power for ignition, there have been occasions where drive belts have had to be changed in the field. The 956s also carried additional fittings, such as an extra pair of headlights, which are not required in daylight-only sprint races. The three Le Mans 956s, numbered 1, 2 and 3, recorded scrutineering weights of 858, 866 and 868kg respectively.

The first Le Mans race produced a dream result; first, second and third, from three starters. The winning car ran almost trouble-free throughout, but it did suffer a puncture, and also required some short stops to adjust the fuel injection mixture settings. Car number two also had a relatively reliable run, although it too required attention to the fuel mixture, and also needed clutch adjustments. The third car suffered delays totalling over an hour, after a wheel bearing broke up, and damaged the left rear suspension; the fact that the car could remain stationary for over an hour and still be in third position at the end is an indication of the level of the opposition which faced the 956s.

Winning at Le Mans is a tremendous boost for a team, but it can have its drawbacks. The 956, and its descendant, the 962, were extremely successful, but this success resulted in less money being made available than the engineers would have liked (but then, car builders and teams always would like more money). The attitude of a winning company can quite often be that if the car can win Le Mans, and every other trophy that's available, then quite clearly it does not need much spending on it. In the case of the 956, there was a lot of truth in that, for a very long time.

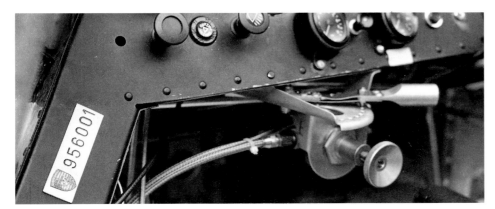

PORSCHE 962

The 962 was conceived as an IMSA GTP version of the 956. The major difference was the engine while the chassis had a lengthened wheelbase to bring the pedals behind the front wheel axis and a steel roll cage, both later becoming mandatory in Group C also. Consequently, the GTP chassis was equipped with a 9 Group C engine for 1985 onwards. Before that, in 1984 the Fitzpatrick team ran its own IMSA to Group C engine conversion at Le Mans but the car crashed during the race. The same year a GTP-spec. 962 was run at Le Mans by the Preston Henn team but expired with four hours to run.

The 'official' 962C arrived at Le Mans in 1985, the factory running three examples with larger diameter rear wheels for bigger venturi tunnels. A further two examples were privately entered. The factory cars qualified first, thrid and fifth but were outrun by the Joest and Lloyd 956s in the race. Bell/Stuck came home third while Ickx/Mass were tenth after gearbox problems and Schuppan/Holbert/Watson retired with engine failure. Of the private entries, the Brun car crashed after transmission failure while the Kremer example came home ninth.

In 1986 Le Mans again saw three works 962Cs and that driven by Bell/Stuck/Holbert won, though the other two examples retired (accident and transmission failure). Of three private entries, the Brun car of Larrauri/Gouhier/Pareja finished second.

With the 956 no longer eligible, 13 962Cs were entered for Le Mans in 1987. Three works cars ran 3.0 litre engines while the privateers had 2.8 litre versions. A number of private cars were based around replacement aluminium honeycomb monocoques. Poor fuel was blamed for a spate of early race retirements, including the works car of Wollek/Mass/Schuppan which lasted only 16 laps. Fortunately a chip change was carried out quickly enough to save the Bell/Stuck/Holbert car which fought off a strong Jaguar challenge. The private 962C of the Obermaier team driven by Laessig/Yver/de Dryver finished second.

Three works 962Cs arrived at Le Mans in 1988 equipped with an improved Bosch engine mangement system offering an extra 50 bhp with improved fuel economy. A titanic struggle with the TWR Jaguar team finally went to the ever improving rival. The Wollek/Schuppan/van der Merwe works 962C led for six hours only for its engine to break just before 3 am. while the Bell/Stuck/Ludwig car was second at the finish only one minute adrift. More than that had been lost early on when Ludwig ran out of fuel and had to return to the pits on the ignition. The third works car finished sixth running on five cylinders. The private 962C fleet was led home by the Joest 962C of Jelinski/Dickens/'Winter' in third place.

PORSCHE	
962C - 1985	Boxer 6
Aluminium monocoque	2.6 litres
Suspension:	Alloy blocks
wishbone front	Fuel injected
rocker arm rear	24 valves
Engine semi-stressed	d.o.h.c.
Porsche gearbox	Twin turbo
Ground effect car	650b.h.p.

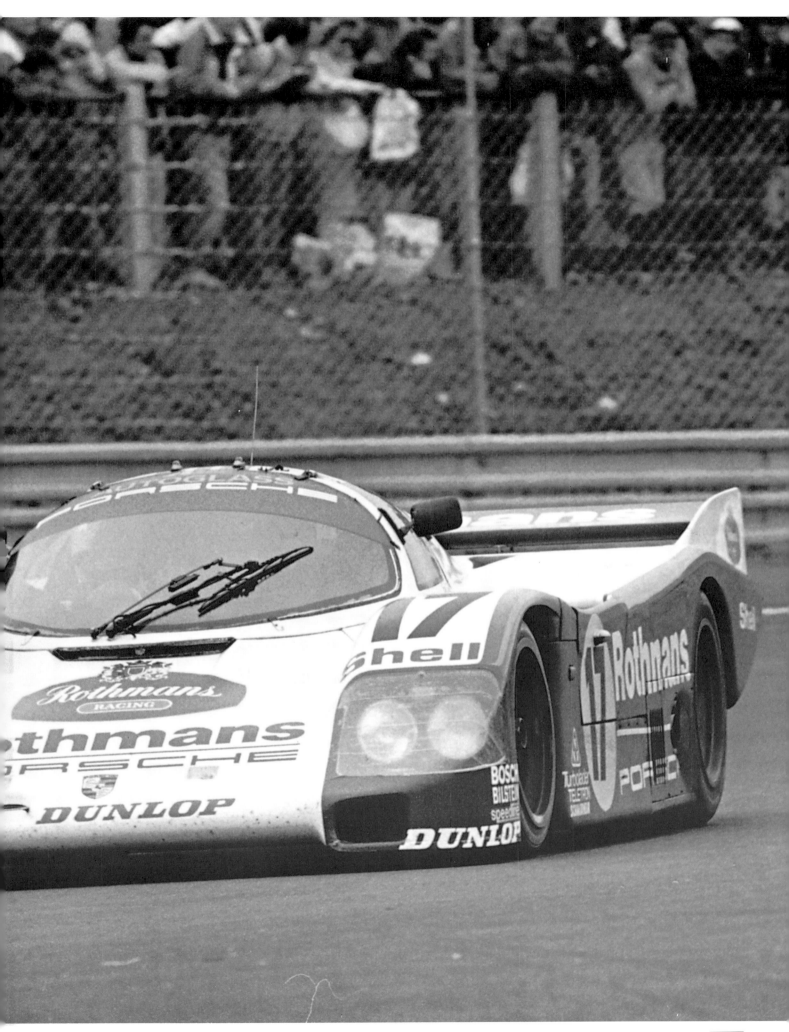

DOME TOYOTA 85-88

Toyota's first attempt at Le Mans was a low key effort in 1980 when its turbocharged Celica failed to qualify. The company did not come back until 1985.

In 1983 a Group C Toyota prototype was unveiled with a chassis produced by the Dome company and a four cylinder Toyota turbo engine. The project was developed over two seasons of national racing prior to Le Mans where one car was run by Dome, another by TOMS, both factory backed.

The chassis was a carbon fibre and Kevlar monocoque with rocker arm rear suspension setting the dampers over the transaxle. Cooling provision set a water radiator in the nose, oil and intercoolers in the flanks. The g.r.p. body incorporated a nose splitter to control the airflow to the underwing while a rear wing was supported by two heafty tail fins.

The engine was a 2090cc. in line unit derived from the production Celica with two valve belt driven heads. Boosted at 1.5 bar by a twin entry turbocharger, power was quoted as 500 bhp. A Nippon Denso engine management system was fitted. Lack of power saw the cars left behind though the TOMS entry finished, in 12th place. Clutch failure sidelined the Dome car.

The two teams were back in 1986 with aerodynamically revised, narrower front track cars carrying revised engines and a March rather than a Hewland transmission.

Overall, the package was 30 kg. lighter. The cars again looked short of power and the TOMS entry went out with engine failure in the eighth hour. The Dome chassis looked set for an 11th place finish but the turbocharger caught fire with less than an hour to run.

For 1987 the introduction of a new 16 valve head increased power to 680 bhp, the engine now known as the 3S GT and displacing 2140 cc. The wheelbase was 10 cm. longer and subtle aerodynamic changes had been made. The 87C was another 20 kg. lighter. This year both entries were from TOMS, now the full factory team. Low on top speed, the cars qualified 14th and 16th and both retired: out of fuel and head gasket failure.

The TOMS cars came back in 1988 with suspension and cooling revisions and qualified in the top 10 and finished, 12th and 24th after various delays.

DOME	TOYOTA
85C - 1985	in line 4
Composite monocoque	2.1 litres
Suspension:	Iron block
wishbone front	Fuel injected
rocker arm rear	8 valves
Engine semi-stressed	s.o.h.c.
Hewland gearbox	Single turbo
Ground effect car	500b.h.p.

Group 6 regulations were relaxed for the category's final season, 1981, allowing the use of engines larger than 3.0 litres and the ACO received an entry from the Kremer Brothers of a Porsche 917K. Based on a Kremer produced spaceframe built from factory drawings, the car was supplied by the factory with 4.5 and 4.9 litre 917 engines. The bodywork reflected more recent areodynamic thinking, however, the car having a longer, gradually tapered nose and a flatter rear deck across the rear of which was a full width aerofoil. After 10 years, the factory assisted car can be considered a 'refresher course' in coupe aerodynamics.

Alas, the Kremer 917K was bugged by problems and although it ran competitively in Wollek's hands in the early stages of the race, it was crashed at quater distance by a co-driver. Another curiosity of the 1981 race was Max Sardou's Ardex S80 coupe which mounted a BMW M1 engine alongside the driver. The idea of abandoning the traditional mid engine layout was to make room for larger venturi tunnels

but the ground effect worked too well: the car was slow on the straight and failed to qualify.

Another coupe that failed to start in 1981 was the Z&W Chevrolet GTP car. This turned out to be an old McLaren M12 chassis equipped with an M6GT g.r.p. body. Poorly prepared, the 5.7 litre Chevrolet V8 engined machine was slowest of all in qualifying.

A more impressive American entry that came closer to starting was the Mirage M12-DFL entered by Grand Touring Cars of Scottsdale, Arizona. Based on a Tiga aluminium honeycomb monocoque, the model had been produced by John Horsman. Horsman's Gulf Research Racing (Mirage) team had been bought by Harley Cluxton in

1975 and the team proprietor arranged a powerful driver line up for two entries which included Mario Andretti and Rick Mears.

Only one car was completed in time for the race and this was qualified by Andretti and his son Michael in an excellent ninth place. Alas, shortly before the race it was noticed that the oil cooler was illegally mounted behind the gearbox and the car was disqualified in spite of the fact that the scrutineers had accepted it earlier in the day. Cluxton's team didn't return to Le Mans...

From 1983 onwards a second division Group C category was run, initially known as Group C Junior, then as C2. A tighter fuel allowance restricted engine performance but otherwise regulations were similar. At first the class was monopolised in terms of Le Mans results by Mazda rotary engined cars, a works chassis winning in 1983 while an American entered Lola-Mazda was victorious in 1984. In 1985 Gordon Spice Racing took the first of a series of wins with a 3.3 DFL powered Tiga.A similarly engined Gebhardt won Le Mans in 1986 then Spice came back to claim the '87 and '88 honours using its own chassis.

CHASSIS INDEX

This is a complete listing of the chassis profiled in the 1964 - '71 and '80 - '88 sections, togther with identification of the accompanying photographs detailing year and drivers.